Shropshire's Oddities

Dorothy Nicolle

GET Publishing

This book is dedicated to my father, Duncomb Walker.
It was Dad who gave me my love of my country and its history.
Dad had a wry sense of humour
and delighted in the quirkiness of much that he saw around him
and I know he would have enjoyed sharing these oddities with me.
He was, and still is, my constant inspiration.

Front cover photos (clockwise from top left):
Grecian Temple, Badger Dingle; Green man carving, Stokesay Castle;
Milestone, Shrewsbury; Sundial, Benthall Church;
Buck's Head sign, Wem.
Back cover:
Standing stone, Mitchell's Fold

ISBN 978-0-9548793-8-9

Published by
GET Publishing, 57 Queens Road, Bridgnorth, Shropshire WV15 5DG

Printed by
Hobbs the Printers Ltd., Brunel Road, Totton, Hampshire SO40 3WX

CONTENTS

Page

5 Introduction

6 1 Natural oddities
Places to visit: Ashford Carbonell, Aston-on-Clun, Boscobel, Bromlow Callow,
Church Preen, Claverley, Coalport, Cressage, Dudleston, Long Mynd, Lydbury
North, Norbury, Quatford, Shrewsbury, Uppington

13 2 Our pagan ancestry
Places to visit: Acton Burnell, Battlefield, Black Marsh Circle, Church Stretton,
Holdgate, Linley, Middleton-in-Chirbury, Mitchell's Fold Circle, More, Sellatyn,
Stokesay Castle, Tugford, Uppington, Wroxeter

18 3 Early Christians and their holy places
Places to visit: Bitterley, Donington, Mainstone, Much Wenlock, Oswestry, Stoke St
Milborough, Tibberton, Woolston

23 4 Church buildings
Places to visit: Alberbury, Astley, Bettws-y-crwyn, Chirbury, Cleobury Mortimer,
Clun, Culmington, Heath, Hodnet, Ironbridge, Lea Cross, Llanyblodwel, Longnor,
Ludlow, Lydbury North, Maesbury, Minsterley, Poynton, Sambrook, Shrewsbury,
Stapleton, Telford, Tong, Wellington, Worthen

31 5 Inside churches
Places to visit: Acton Burnell, Astley Abbots, Bettws-y-crwyn, Bromfield, Burford,
Cheswardine, Claverley, Cleobury Mortimer, Cound, Edstaston, Longnor, Melverley,
Middleton-in-Chirbury, Minsterley, Moreton Corbet, Morville, Myddle, Shifnal, St
Martin's, Stokesay, Whitchurch

39 6 Public buildings
Places to visit: Alveley, Bishop's Castle, Boscobel, Bridgnorth, Horsehay, Ironbridge,
Ludlow, Morville, Much Wenlock, Norton, Oswestry, Prees, Shrewsbury, Wem,
Weston-under-Redcastle

53 7 Clocks
Places to visit: Alveley, Benthall, Knockin, Lilleshall, Llanymynech, Lydbury North,
Madeley, Shrewsbury, Telford

57 8 Animals
Places to visit: Beckbury, Benthall, Caynham, Craven Arms, Hodnet, Loppington,
Lydbury North, Middleton-in-Chirbury, Much Wenlock, Rudge, St Martin's,
Shipton, Shrewsbury, Tong, Wollerton

62 9 Borders and boundaries
Places to visit: Llanymynech, Norton in Hales, Offa's Dyke, Oswestry, Shrewsbury,
Thresholds, Whitchurch

67   10   Along the roadside
Places to visit: All Stretton, Alveley, Bishop's Castle, Blist's Hill, Bridgnorth, Craven Arms, Ellesmere, Little Brampton, Ludlow, Minsterley, Montford, Oswestry, Priorslee, Shrewsbury

75   11   Odd signs
Places to visit: Broseley, Homer, Knockin, Melverley, New Invention, Oswestry, Shrewsbury, The Bog, Wigwig

78   12   Earliest houses
Places to visit: Blist's Hill, Boscobel, Bridgnorth, Haughmond, Ludlow, Much Wenlock, Nesscliffe, Shrewsbury

83   13   Later domestic buildings
Places to visit: Atcham, Benthall, Felhampton, Ludlow, Madeley, Much Wenlock, Shrewsbury, Upton Magna, Wem

92   14   Gardens and gazebos
Places to visit: Atcham, Boscobel, Eyton-upon-Severn, Shrewsbury

95   15   Industrial Revolution
Places to visit: Bridgnorth, Cantlop Bridge, Coalbrookdale, Coalport, Hadley, Ironbridge, Longdon-on-Tern, Madeley, Morville, Newport, Shrewsbury, Whitchurch, Whixall

102   16   Other industrial survivals
Places to visit: Bridgnorth, Eardington, Hampton Loade, Leighton, Shrewsbury, Snailbeach, Wem, Wenlock Edge

106   17   The 20th century
Places to visit: Cressage, Ebury Hill, Ellesmere, Market Drayton, Nesscliffe, Titterstone Clee

109   18   Follies
Places to visit: Badger Dingle, Hadnall, Haughmond Hill, Hodnet, Wenlock Edge, Weston Rhyn, Weston-under-Redcastle

112   19   And finally, some unusual graves and memorials
Places to visit: Bettws-y-crwyn, Bridgnorth, Church Stretton, Clive, Coalbrookdale, Haughmond, Moreton Say, Shirlett Forest, Shrewsbury, Stoke-on-Tern, Tong, Welshampton

INTRODUCTION

I have always been fascinated by oddities. For some years now I have been giving talks on local history and have often drawn the attention of my audiences to strange or unusual features around Shropshire.

This book is the result of those lectures, in which I have also tried to encourage local people to explore the wonderful county in which we live. I would like to take this opportunity to thank all those who have told me of their own favourite oddities and so have contributed to this collection, and to the friends who have commented on my manuscript as it grew and whose advice I have occasionally followed.

Oddities come in all types. Anything that is a little bit out of the ordinary will be considered odd by some people. Some are simply natural features but are rare or just look curious; some are things that were once considered normal but seem weird to us; and still others were deliberately built to appear strange.

I have broken them down into groups under chapter headings without any regard to their location. For those of you who wish to seek them out for yourselves, I would suggest that you have a few target sites in the area you intend to explore and then go searching. You will need an Ordnance Survey map to find many of them, and I have given map references for some of those in the countryside and near villages. The first three numbers of each map reference refer to the Ordnance Survey Landranger map. I would warn you that some of the oddities require a bit of footwork and searching out.

Please note that many of the oddities in the book are on private land. Sometimes these can be seen from the road or a public right of way. A few, however, are not accessible to the public, and where this is the case I have not given any directions at all.

Happy hunting!

1 NATURAL ODDITIES

Whitchurch
Dudleston
Oswestry
Shrewsbury
Telford
Uppington
Boscobel
Bromlow Callow · Cressage · Coalport
Long Mynd
Norbury · Church Preen · Bridgnorth
Linley
Claverley
Bishop's Castle
Quatford
Lydbury North · Aston on Clun
Clun
Knighton
Ludlow
Ashford Carbonell

At first glance the Belstone, sitting by the entrance to the Morris Hall off Barker Street in Shrewsbury, seems to be nothing more than a lump of granite. In fact its existence in Shrewsbury is curious, for it is what's known as an *erratic*. Erratics are stones (and they can sometimes be huge, the size of a large truck or more) that have been moved from one place to another by ice during the Ice Age. This one came from Cumbria and was deposited here when the ice eventually melted.

There is another reason why this stone is of special interest. The story of how it moved all the way from Cumbria to Shropshire was told in the early 19th century to a young Shrewsbury boy who was interested in all aspects of natural history and geology. That young boy was Charles Darwin and it was probably one of the many things that helped to ignite his interest in all aspects of the natural world.

Another interesting geological phenomenon in Shropshire is the tar tunnel (127 694026) in Coalport. It was found quite by accident when a tunnel to take wagons under the hill to nearby coal-workings was dug in 1786. The sides of the tunnel began to ooze with a tarry oil – 1,000 gallons a week at one time – and so it was worked commercially and the oil exported all over Europe. Eventually, one hundred years later, it was worked out, and the tunnel returned to its intended use transporting coal to barges on the River Severn.

Today it has become a most unusual tourist attraction.

Despite its name the Boiling Well near the top of Long Mynd (137 421946) doesn't boil at all. It's simply a natural spring.

The land around it, however, is turf and air has been trapped within the soil just above the water table which at this point is very close to the surface. Jump up and down on the turf beside the spring, and bubbles of air will appear in the water as though it were boiling. But you must choose the right conditions: in very wet weather the ground can be so waterlogged that no amount of jumping will produce bubbles!

Which is the oldest tree in the country? Beside the yew tree in the churchyard at Church Preen there is a plaque that tells us that it started life in "approx 457AD". Don't you just love that word "approx"! Assuming that the date is reasonably accurate, this would make the tree over 1,550 years old. However, yew trees are notoriously difficult to date. This is because, as they grow outwards over the centuries, their cores rot away. Consequently, dating them depends largely on guesswork and estimates according to their girth and probable rate of growth.

There are a number of other ancient yews in Shropshire. There's one for instance in the churchyard at Claverley that's said to be 2,500 years old; others can be found in Norbury, Uppington (pictured overleaf), Ashford Carbonell and Dudleston. The last of these is hollow and was used for a short time to house the church bell – the church tower was being repaired at the time and so the bell was hung from one of the upper branches of the tree.

The fact that all these yews are in churchyards is because our pagan ancestors worshipped the tree. They, too, were aware of its longevity and it would therefore appear that many of our early Christian churches were sited deliberately in pagan sacred groves where yews were already growing. Although poisonous, the yews were allowed to continue growing because their wood was needed for the production of bows – the wood of the yew is particularly pliant when subjected to stress and the best longbows were always made from yew.

Have you ever wondered why, in this country, a particularly rude gesture is made using two fingers whereas the equivalent gesture in other parts of the world is always made with only one finger? There is a reason for this: during the Hundred Years War between England and France English archers were supreme. However, if an English longbowman was taken prisoner by the enemy he was liable to be mutilated by having two of his fingers removed, the two fingers on his right hand that held the arrow steady as he drew his bow. Without those fingers he would be rendered useless as an archer. Consequently, whenever English soldiers met the French and wanted to show they were quite capable of taking up arms, they would show them that they still had their two fingers. And so the gesture that later acquired more vulgar connotations took root.

But it's not just Shropshire's yew trees that can be considered unusual. There are a number of particularly old oak trees too, many of which have legends attached to them. One is the Cressage Oak (126 582047): legend has it that this tree, in a field beside the road to Shrewsbury, will never die. It's associated with St Samson, a Welshman who went to study Christianity in Ireland in the 6th century. On his return he became a hermit somewhere "on the banks of the River Severn". But where? It must have been somewhere reasonably remote, and since the original church for this village was named after him, tradition has it that it was here that he stayed.

St Samson preached in this area and probably sheltered under oak trees as he did so and this, in fact, is where Cressage gets its name – *Christ's oak*. Today "the tree that will never die" is the only preaching tree left but is obviously far too young to have ever sheltered the saint. But look at it closely and you will see that the present tree is actually growing almost from within the trunk of a much older tree – so, in one sense, the legend could be said to be true.

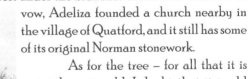

Incidentally, St Samson moved on from here to become a missionary in Cornwall before going to Brittany where he founded the monastery at Dol and eventually became Brittany's patron saint.

But there are a number of genuinely old oak trees within the county, one of which is the Quatford Oak (below) (138 743908). Soon after the Battle of Hastings in 1066 William the Conqueror sent his general, Roger de Montgomery, to the Shropshire area to control the borders of his new territory. Having arrived here, Roger sent to Normandy for his wife, Adeliza. While crossing the English Channel, Adeliza was so terrified by a storm that she prayed to God to save her and everyone with her. She promised that, should she reach England safely, she would establish a church wherever she met her husband. Roger was out hunting in the forest near Bridgnorth when Adeliza arrived, and they met in the forest under the branches of this tree. True to her

vow, Adeliza founded a church nearby in the village of Quatford, and it still has some of its original Norman stonework.

As for the tree – for all that it is certainly quite old, I doubt that it is old enough to be the actual tree under the branches of which Roger and Adeliza met all those years ago. But it's a good story.

Another oak, in this case one that is associated with a well known story, is the Boscobel Oak (127 837081) in which Charles II hid when he was on the run following his defeat at the Battle of

9

Worcester in 1651. Charles hid in priest holes within the house at Boscobel during the night, and hid in the tree during the day while, all around him, the Parliamentarian soldiers searched. It's a hard story to believe when you look at the tree today, but like the oak tree at Cressage, Boscobel's oak is actually a descendant of the original tree. Furthermore, it stands on its own in the middle of a field, and even a squirrel would have difficulty hiding within it today. But the farmland all around was once a hunting forest, and in the 1600s the oak tree would have been one of many hundreds of trees in thick woodland – making it a much more secure hiding place.

It's noteworthy that, after he regained his throne in 1660, Charles II remembered the five brothers at Boscobel who had helped him escape and he arranged for an annual payment of £320 to be shared between them – an enormous sum of money in those days. Not only was this money to be paid to the brothers themselves but it was to be paid to their descendants in perpetuity. With so many descendants over the generations, the individual sums have become smaller and smaller – but they still continue to be paid!

When Charles II came back to England in 1660 he arrived on Oak Apple Day (29 May), and because by then many people had heard the story of how he had hidden in the oak tree they celebrated his arrival by wearing sprigs of oak leaves on the lapels of their coats. For years, on Oak Apple Day people would also decorate trees in celebration.

This tradition survives in Shropshire, but not with an oak tree. It's a black poplar in the centre of Aston on Clun that is decorated every year. It was in 1786, by which time the tradition had died out in most places, that a local man, John Marston, married Mary Carter. After the wedding the couple drove through the village in their carriage, and Mary was delighted to see the tree covered in flags. Thinking this had been done to celebrate their wedding, Mary then arranged for money to be put aside to ensure that the tradition continued. To this day, therefore, on the last Sunday of May each year, the tree in Aston (opposite page, top) is decorated. Yet again, it's no longer the original tree – that one fell down in 1995.

Another tree that was once considered very unusual was the larch. In the 18th century Robert More of Linley Hall and the Duke of Atholl, both keen botanists, were rivals to see which of them could bring larches home from Austria and so plant the first ones in this country – Robert More won, planting his the day before the Duke. Descendants of these first larches still grow in the grounds of the hall. Before long everyone was following suit, so that William Wordsworth was later to comment that he deplored the fact that these "foreign conifers" were starting to cover our hillsides.

Since larches are deciduous trees, when planted amongst other fir trees, they can make interesting markers. One such marker can be seen each autumn on the A488 road that links Clun with Knighton: just to the north of Knighton the letters ER (137 296730) stand out clearly on the hillside – these were originally planted to commemorate the Queen's coronation in 1953.

Another such marker can be found in woodland near to Lydbury North – this time the name ROY (137 370843) can sometimes be distinguished. This, however, is a memorial to a man of that name who died there.

But the best such marker has long gone. In 1763 Robert Clive purchased the estate of Walcot Hall, also near Lydbury North. He, of course, had made an immense fortune through his victories in India and, to commemorate his most successful battle he planted trees on the estate to spell out the word PLASSEY.

By the mid 20th century these trees had become so well-established that during the Second World War RAF pilots used the "Plassey" trees as a landmark. But it was soon realised that if our boys could use them, so could the enemy, and, sadly, they were promptly felled.

Trees have also often been used as special meeting points, giving rise to a number of villages called Acton (the settlement by the oak tree) or Ashton (ash tree) for example. One particularly distinctive clump of trees that can be seen from miles away is the group of pine trees on Bromlow Callow (126 325011) south-west of Minsterley – they are said to have been markers for a drovers' route indicating the way for men driving their cattle from Wales to the livestock market in Shrewsbury.

OUR PAGAN ANCESTRY 2

All people need a religion even if nowadays many seem to worship on Sundays at the altar of the god of shopping! Trying to fully understand the religious beliefs of our pre-Christian ancestors is impossible, nor can we ever know for sure just how our ancestors practised their religions. This makes it hard for us to understand the many strange monuments that must once have been associated with ancient religious ceremonies.

The most obvious such monuments are standing stones, both single and in groups or circles. The best-known such group of stones in Shropshire is Mitchell's Fold (137 304984) on a hill overlooking the A488 between Minsterley and Bishop's Castle.

Inevitably stories arose in order to explain how these monuments were built, and the legend associated with Mitchell's Fold is delightful. Once upon a time, so the story goes, a good fairy came to the local people. The fairy understood that it was hard to make a living in the hills, and so she brought the people a "dun" or brown cow and said that if each housewife took just one bucket of milk a day from the cow then their futures would be assured and they would never starve.

It shall not fail if but one pail
Each wife shall daily draw.

13

But the inevitable happened and a wicked witch turned up. She followed the rules and just brought one bucket, and she began to milk the cow. But no matter how hard that poor cow tried, she just couldn't fill the bucket because, you see, the wicked witch had brought a bucket with a hole in the bottom. In the end the poor cow went berserk and ran off, to be killed eventually, so it is said, by Earl Guy a fair distance away in Warwickshire. The good fairy returned and magically erected the stone circle in order to imprison the wicked witch within it forevermore.

Today it's difficult to make out the full circle of stones – only 15 stones survive of the original number (there may have been as many as 30 altogether) erected some 3,500 years ago. Incidentally, if you visit Mitchell's Fold, don't miss the little church at Middleton-in-Chirbury (137 298993) on the western side of the hill. Inside the church there is a wonderful collection of carvings, some of which show scenes from the legend of Mitchell's Fold with the wicked witch clearly defined by her tall witch's hat as she sits milking the cow.

There's a second stone circle to the north of Mitchell's Fold known as the Black Marsh Circle (137 324999). If you study this circle you will see that one stone has strange holes carved into it – these cavities are relatively modern and were made by miners setting off gunpowder to celebrate local weddings.

As for solitary standing stones, there's a fine one near Sellatyn (126 255329) in the hills beyond Oswestry (below left).

When the Romans arrived in this country in AD 43 they brought their many gods with them. Not much evidence survives of these (in Shropshire at least), but there is one Roman altar in the churchyard at Uppington (below right). The altar was found in 1678 in the ground near where it now stands not far, of course, from the ancient Roman town of Viroconium known today as Wroxeter.

However, there are a number of other Roman curiosities surviving in our churches. For many centuries the water for babies being baptised in St Andrew's Church in Wroxeter was contained in a font (opposite page, top) made from the base of an old Roman column. Not only is the font made from an old column but two more Roman columns flank the entrance to the churchyard. This church does, after all, sit within the boundaries of Viroconium.

Another Roman survival in a church is a small section of a Roman mosaic floor (below) that can be found in St Peter's at More. It adorns the plinth for the font and was brought here after being dug up from an old Roman villa in the grounds of nearby Linley Hall.

Christianity arrived in Britain during the time of the Roman Empire but, with the abandonment of Britannia by the Romans even those Britons who had been converted nearly all reverted to their old pagan ways. Again, we know little of the pagan beliefs of the time but a few small carvings survive and the most fascinating thing about them is that some of them can be found incorporated within later Christian churches.

These carvings are known as *sheila-na-gigs*. They are crude (in every sense of the word) little female figures and must have been associated with fertility rites of some sort. Presumably, when our ancestors were converted to Christianity and began to build their early churches, some of the carvings were then incorporated within the new buildings – we can never entirely abandon our old gods after all. Over the centuries (especially during Puritan times) many would have been covered up or hidden in one way or another so that it's interesting to speculate how many there may be hidden within our churches to this day that we are totally unaware of.

There's a sheila-na-gig to be found on the north wall of St Lawrence's Church in Church Stretton (right), another on the south wall of the church at Holdgate. St Catherine's at Tugford has two sheila-na-gigs and they sit just inside the church over the south door.

The church at Acton Burnell has a number of carvings around the exterior, one of which depicts an exceptionally well-endowed gentleman (right). Beside him there's another carving which is seriously eroded but could, with a little imagination, perhaps be another sheila-na-gig.

The importance of fertility, for humans, livestock or crops is shown by the need for gods associated with it. Examples of images associated with fertility can be found in carvings of green men. These are usually carvings of a male face with foliage growing from the mouth and one of the most beautiful such carvings can be found on the gatehouse at Stokesay Castle (left).

Green men can also be found in many of our churches – there's a fine one in Battlefield Church for example. Yet another (in this case it's a carving not just of the face but of the whole man standing with his legs apart) decorates a 12th century tympanum on the north wall of the little church of St Leonard's in Linley not far from Bridgnorth.

3 EARLY CHRISTIANS AND THEIR HOLY PLACES

Following the arrival of St Augustine in Kent at the end of the 6th century missionaries began to spread the word of God around the country once again. A number of places soon came to be closely associated with particular saints and prime amongst these are the numerous holy wells to be found all around Shropshire.

The prettiest of them must be the one dedicated to St Winifred at Woolston (126 323244). The association arose because it was here that her bones rested for one night while being transported from Snowdonia to Shrewsbury Abbey in 1137. The water from the well rises to the surface in a small spring and it's supposed to be excellent for curing eye complaints. Occasionally, however, the water appears to be stained red "from Winifred's blood" – more likely there is iron in the soil locally.

In medieval times people would travel from far and wide to visit holy wells so that small markets and communities grew up owing their prosperity entirely to pilgrims visiting their well. St Winifred's Well was no exception. A cottage was built above the spring and from around 1600 this building was used as a courthouse. It was probably needed because, during the summer months (the season for pilgrimage), temporary alehouses were established and who knows what might happen with large groups of people on pilgrimage (the holidays of medieval times) and drinking to excess!

Today the little cottage has been restored by the Landmark Trust and is used for holiday lets.

The Venerable Bede, writing in the early 8th century, talks of St Oswald's holy well in his *History of the English Church and People*. This well is to be found in Oswestry in Oswald's Well Road. King Oswald of Northumbria  (a Christian) was killed in battle near here while fighting against the pagan King Penda of Mercia. Following the battle, Oswald's body was mutilated, cut up into pieces and the pieces hung in a tree – this is where the town gets its name – *Oswald's tree* or Oswestry. An eagle flying by came down to the tree, picked up a limb from the King's body and flew off with it before dropping it a short distance away. Where the limb struck the ground a spring miraculously arose – Oswald's Well. As a Christian king killed by a pagan, King Oswald was soon venerated as a saint and before long pilgrims came to the miraculous well where, so Bede tells us, many "sick men and beasts are healed to this day". A number of these people took away a souvenir of their visit – a small cupful of earth from beside the well. According to Bede "this practice became so popular that, as the earth was gradually removed, a pit was left in which a man could stand". This, presumably, explains the hollow area in front of the spring.

One saint, St Milburga, has two holy wells in Shropshire dedicated to her – one in Much Wenlock and the other in Stoke St Milborough. In fact in Much Wenlock there is confusion as to which of two wells is the correct one. The well (right) normally associated with this saint is beside an unnamed lane off Barrow Street, nearly opposite the Raven Hotel. However, an early map of the town names the well in St Milburga Row as being St Milburga's Well.

St Milburga was a beautiful young maiden who one day, so the story goes, was out riding in the countryside when she was chased by two bloodhounds. They chased her for two days and two nights until eventually Milburga fell from her horse. She lay dying of thirst until her horse kicked at the ground and, miraculously, a well appeared.

Milburga quenched her thirst and then managed to escape. This well is still to be found in the little village that now bears her name – Stoke St Milborough (138 568824).

Some of the saints whose names are associated with local wells came from distant lands. One such well in Queen Street, Much Wenlock, (below) is dedicated to St Owen. He was a French bishop and it is quite possible that he visited St Milburga when she was Abbess of the original abbey here. (If you have ever visited Jersey you may have been to St Ouen's Bay – different spelling and pronunciation but

the same saint.) Then there's a well (and a church) dedicated to St Cuthbert at Donington in Albrighton. St Cuthbert is closely associated with the monastery at Lindisfarne on the other side of England and there's no tradition of his ever having visited the area, but who knows...

All of these wells are reputed to have healing properties. It's worth bearing in mind that this association with wells and healing probably came about for good reason. Today we can get good quality drinking water every time we turn on the tap but then the only clean and safe water would have been from springs. In other words there would have been no better water than spring water for washing wounds.

In fact at the holy well near Tibberton (127 687218) the spring water flows into what appears to be a large concrete and brick basin, which was built just so that people seeking a cure could more easily enter the waters to bathe.

Apart from wells another relic that dates from the earliest times of the Christian church is the Mainstone. It's a great granite boulder weighing around 230 lbs (105kilos), another erratic like the Belstone in Shrewsbury. But this stone also has a religious association. The legend associated with the stone tells us how, when they were first converted to Christianity, the villagers decided to build a church. They wanted this new church to be down in the valley near to their houses rather than where their old pagan ceremonial centre was. The stone sat in their pagan site, however, and in order perhaps to please those people who weren't too sure about changing to this new religion, it was decided that it should be taken to the new church as well. It was brought down the hill and the villagers began work on building their church. At the end of the day they all went home but when they returned the next morning they found that the stone had disappeared. They searched and found it up the hill at the old site – it had apparently moved there of its own accord during the night.

They brought the stone down into the valley once more and continued working on the new church. That night, while they slept, the stone rolled back up the hill once more so that they had once again to fetch it the following morning. This happened over several nights so that eventually the villagers got the message – the stone was insisting that the new Christian church should be built on the old pagan religious site.

This explains why Mainstone's church lies some distance from the heart of the community to this day. Incidentally the name comes from a Welsh word *maen* which simply means *stone*.

Another relic that appears to link Christianity with earlier beliefs is the stone cross that stands in the churchyard at Bitterley. It has a hole that has been drilled right through it and this is said to be a sighting hole for a ley line. The country is covered with these lines which were discovered in the 1920s by Alfred Watkins who came from Hereford. Ley lines are alignments linking ancient holy places and can sometimes run for distances of many miles linking numerous prehistoric sites such as standing stones, stone circles, burial mounds and even many Christian churches. Their purpose? Who knows? Some people say they were used for ancient traders' routes but since they go up and down some extremely steep slopes this seems unlikely. Some even say they are navigational aids for UFOs!

This particular ley line is said to link up with the peak of Brown Clee Hill to the north and the churches at Stoke Prior and Hope-under-Dinmore in Herefordshire to the south.

CHURCH BUILDINGS 4

Map of Shropshire showing:
Whitchurch, Oswestry, Hodnet, Sambrook, Maesbury, Llanyblodwel, Astley, Poynton, Alberbury, Shrewsbury, Telford, Lea Cross, Wellington, Stapleton, Ironbridge, Tong, Worthen, Minsterley, Longnor, Chirbury, Bridgnorth, Bishop's Castle, Heath, Lydbury North, Clun, Culmington, Bettws-y-crwyn, Cleobury Mortimer, Ludlow

Because of their age, churches are often particularly good examples of places where we find things that strike us today as curious but which were once considered perfectly ordinary. Sometimes it's the building itself that is unusual for one reason or another, very often it's a curiosity within the building that is worth seeking out.

Amongst the oldest churches in the county is the one at Stapleton dedicated to St John the Baptist which was built as a two-storey building with the church on the upper floor and an undercroft below. It dates from around 1200, a period when many houses were built in this pattern providing living accommodation for humans on the upper floor and for animals down below.

In 1786 the entire building was remodelled so that the floor between the two levels was removed. This means that today, when you go inside the church, you find the piscina (a recess built into the wall for the washing of Communion vessels), which would normally be no higher than waist height

is now several feet above your head. The entrance to this church would originally have been from an exterior flight of stairs. Another church which still has an exterior flight of stairs (although in this case it only leads to a gallery at the back of the church) is St Mary's in Longnor.

Most churches were first built so that you entered at the west

23

end and looked east towards the altar. St Luke's in Ironbridge (previous page), however, was built the other way around with its main entrance at the east end.

Medieval round churches are very rare, but we have one in Shropshire, for all that only the ruined nave now survives – it was once part of the chapel within the castle at Ludlow (left). Also in Ludlow the parish church of St Laurence's has an unusual hexagonal porch: the only other such porch in England is found in Bristol's St Mary Redcliffe. Even more unusual is the 14th century tower of St Luke's, Hodnet (left) – octagonal from the ground to the top, it's said to be the only one of its kind in the country.

Shropshire is a border county – our Welsh neighbours would often come riding across the border to raid our cattle and plunder our farms!

Consequently, good look-out points were essential and a number of church towers reflect this. The best examples of towers that were definitely built with a military purpose in mind include those attached to the churches at Clun (left), Worthen and perhaps the one at Alberbury.

A particularly unusual (and much later) spire is the one for St Michael's Church at Llanyblodwel. This one only dates from the 1850s and was built by the vicar at a cost of £1,529.13.0. It looks just like a rocket waiting to be launched. Another even more recent spire is to be found on All Saints Church at Culmington. Apparently the original one was never finished and so it was capped with a temporary lid made from lead. The new one, really an aluminium frame, was finally finished in 1969/70 and was hoisted into position by a helicopter.

But the most unusual spire in the county has to be the one on St Mary's Church in Cleobury Mortimer (right) which is crooked. Actually such spires aren't really that unusual but they are fun to look out for. Spires were built from wooden frames that were then covered with wooden shingles or slates. It was the norm, however, to build them using green, unseasoned timber. Over the years the timbers then dried out and, as they dried, they warped and twisted so that the entire steeple became distorted.

Mind you, it's not just the steeple at Cleobury Mortimer that's twisted. Some of the walls appear to lean at really crazy angles. Another church where you feel that the outer walls could collapse at any moment is St Michael's Church at Chirbury (left) – it's rather a relief to go into the churchyard and see, along the outside walls, that there are sturdy buttresses holding the building up.

On the other hand Holy Trinity Church at Minsterley (left) was actually built with its side walls very slightly, but deliberately, out of plumb, leaning inwards to resist the thrust of the roof.

Other unusual churches include St Chad's in Shrewsbury (above). Built in 1790-92 to a design by George Steuart its round shape created a sensation when it was first built and few people in the town were happy with it. Today Shrewsbury's people have grown to love their "salt and mustard pot" – so-named because the tower is said to resemble a salt cellar and the round body of the church a mustard pot. Another unusual feature of the building of this church was the use of iron columns in its structure – it was built, after all, when local ironmasters at nearby Ironbridge were changing the world with their new ideas.

St Mary's Church at Bettws-y-crwyn in the hills of southern Shropshire claims to be one of the highest churches in England. Not high in the religious sense but, rather, in terms of its height above sea level at over 1250 feet (380m). This church originally had a thatched roof, with its attendant risk of

fire. On the outside of the north wall there are two holes for supports for a long pole that would have been kept ready to pull down the thatch should a fire catch hold.

Another similarly lonely church is the beautiful one at Heath (138 557856), one of my favourites in all of Shropshire. Technically it's not a church at all but should be described as a chapel – its purpose was to serve those people nearby who couldn't attend the parish church in Stoke St Milborough.

Many such remote small chapels around the country have long since ceased to function as churches, (and sometimes these little buildings can be

found in areas that are not considered particularly remote these days either). Driving along a country lane in Poynton (126 570179) you will suddenly see an old chapel with a particularly fine traceried three-light window in its gable end. It's now used as a barn.

Some churches in Shropshire have been moved from their original position. One example is the mission church at Blists Hill Victorian Town in Telford (below) which originally served a community of miners and their families living around the nearby Granville Colliery. There's another example of a church that has been moved in Telford's Town Park although this one is a ruin, a ruined Norman chapel. It originally came from Malinslee Hall (or, to be

more precise, the present-day car park area serving Sainsbury's). Probably first built to serve travellers passing through the forest around the Wrekin it now seems to serve more as a climbing frame for young children than as an ancient historic relic. The nave and chancel of this little church were divided by a stone screen part of which can still be seen in the ruins. It was moved here in 1971.

Another interesting church in Telford is one that survived as a place of worship but has changed its denomination somewhat – the former Methodist church at Tan Bank in Wellington (below) has now become a mosque.

An unusual 20th century church is St John's in the village of Maesbury (below). Sometimes described as a "tin tabernacle" it's a genuine church but, like the church at Blist's Hill, was made from corrugated iron; it was built in just three days in 1906.

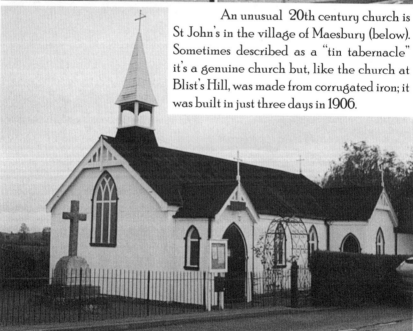

Sometimes churches were built but never consecrated – one example is St Anne's Church at Lea Cross (left) which was built in 1888 by the Revd Hawkes. He had quarrelled with the vicar at nearby Pontesbury and so built a church of his own for his flock. This was subsequently to lead to considerable arguments as to who actually owned the church.

Another unconsecrated church was the little chapel at Sambrook. It was built in 1838 with money raised by subscription amongst the local people and was later replaced when a proper church was built in 1856. While the old chapel was in use baptisms took place using a little iron font (right) which now stands in the churchyard near the west end of the church.

It's not only the church buildings themselves that are unusual. Many people visiting Shrewsbury's Abbey notice the very fine pulpit that sits outside the church on the other side of the road. It is in the correct position – formerly the main road into the town was on the north side of the church and the chapter house, cloisters and refectory of the old abbey sat here. The pulpit would then have been part of the refectory and from here one of the monks would have read to his brothers while the others ate their meals in silence.

Look up at the roof of the north transept of St Laurence's Church in Ludlow and you will see what appears to be an arrow embedded there – it's not a real one, of course. It's known as the Fletcher's Arrow and recalls the fletchers or arrow-makers of medieval times whose guild was within the church.

Further evidence of real arrows can be found on the outside walls of many of our churches. At the time of the Hundred Years War against the French it was our longbowmen who were to save the day in famous battles such as those at Crécy and Agincourt. All men throughout the country were expected to practice their archery every week – indeed, a law was passed that banned the playing of football on Sundays because too many young men and boys were playing football when they should have been practising at the Butts.

While they were waiting they would often hone their arrows on the stone walls of churches, and many buildings have the tell-tale grooves that show where the arrows were sharpened. Perhaps the best example of this is St Mary's Church at Astley (right). But here the grooves may well have had a deadlier purpose – perhaps some of King Henry IV's men sharpened their arrows when they were camped here on the night before the Battle of Shrewsbury in 1403.

Occasionally, a church would find it was right in the thick of a battle. Look out for the bullet holes from the Civil War on St Michael's Church at Lydbury North – they're in the door. St Mary and St Bartholomew's Church (right) at Tong has a number of hollows in its walls – the result of cannonballs hitting the building.

Whitchurch
• St Martin's
• Edstaston
Oswestry
Cheswardine •
Myddle • • Moreton Corbet
• Melverley
Shrewsbury **Telford**
Cound •
Shifnal •
Middleton- Minsterley
in-Chirbury • Acton Burnell •
Longnor • Astley Abbots
Morville • • Claverley
Bishop's Castle **Bridgnorth**
Bettws-y-crwyn • Stokesay
• Bromfield Cleobury Mortimer •
• **Ludlow**
•
Burford

For people who search out oddities there are some real treasures to be found within our churches. Again, sometimes it's part of the building that is special, or it can be the way in which the church has been decorated, or something unusual inside the building.

St Bartholomew's Church at Moreton Corbet, for example, has a section cut out of the inner wall which is claimed to be a leper squint. In medieval times people were terrified of those who suffered from leprosy, a disease for which nothing could then be done. Consequently lepers were given a wide berth and those suffering from the disease had to carry a bell and ring it as a warning for everyone to keep away. But lepers wanted to attend church services and so, occasionally, a small hole would be built into the church through which lepers outside the building could see what was going in within and so be a part of any service.

This one is rather large and, had there been a gap like this in an exterior wall it would have made the building extremely draughty so I'm not too sure about the authenticity of this gap as a true leper squint. Much more likely is the idea that it was built in this way to allow the Corbet family to sit cosily in their private chapel during a service but still have a view of the altar. There's even a fireplace there. But go and see what you think. And when you go, look out also for the welcoming sign on the gate post at the end of the road.

Another possible leper squint can be found in St Mary's Church in Cleobury Mortimer (right). Yet another is to be found in the north side of the chancel at Acton Burnell. However, local tradition has it that this last one was used for an anchorite or religious hermit, although there is no documentary evidence of there ever having been one here.

Another church with a curious feature built into it is St Andrew's in Shifnal where the priest even had a toilet halfway up the stairs.

There are some excellent ancient doors in the county. The modestly sized St Mary's (right), Edstaston, has splendid north and south doors contemporary with their equally splendid late 12th century doorways while the door at St Gregory's at Morville is some 800 years old. Incidentally, there's an unusual story about the day St Gregory's Church was consecrated – apparently there was a terrible storm that day with thunder and lightning and five horses and two women were killed from a lightning strike. What a terrible omen for a new church!

Some rather fine doors are to be found at the entrance to the National Westminster Bank in the High Street in Whitchurch. It's been suggested that they may have come from the old St Alkmund's Church.

Another interesting church door is the one on St Peter's Church at Cound – it has a sanctuary knocker on it. Anyone fleeing from justice could seek refuge by entering a church and reaching the altar or, in this case, by striking the knocker. It sounds a good way to avoid facing up to any punishment for crimes you have committed but it wasn't really that simple. There were rules associated with taking sanctuary – for example it could only last for a certain period, after which you had to leave the security of the church and face the music. The important thing about obtaining sanctuary in a church was that it gave people time to think and so allowed judgements to be reached more fairly once tempers had had a chance to cool down – thus it was an important element in avoiding mob rule.

Many Shropshire churches have wonderful interiors. There's a wall painting that reminds me of the Bayeux Tapestry in Claverley's All Saints Church – it's painted as a narrow strip along the wall, and I'm always convinced when I see it that the artist must have seen the Bayeux Tapestry itself because the whole layout is so similar, with its mounted soldiers all heading off to face their personal battles.

One painted interior that is decidedly curious is to be found on the ceiling of the chancel in St Mary's Church in Bromfield. It is rather late for a painted church interior as it was done in 1672, a time when fashion was dictating that styles should become simpler but it is really quite grotesque. However, it always makes me grin. It reminds me of the fad, a few

years ago, for those distinctly ugly "cabbage patch dolls" with its somewhat chunky cherubs. The chancel ceiling was once memorably described as "the best example of the worst style of ecclesiastical art" – talk about a damning critique.

Another painting that always amuses me is the writing of the Lord's Prayer within St John the Baptist's Church in Stokesay. I know it may seem a strange comment to make but if you go and find it you will discover that someone with what I can only describe as a great sense of self-worth has partially covered it with a family memorial.

There's a fascinating painting to be found in St Mary's Church, Burford. At first it seems quite typical for its period; it's when you see the exact date and consider the political situation of the day that you realise things here aren't quite as they seem. The painting is a triptych – in other words, it's a religious painting, painted on three panels two of which close over to act as doors covering the third panel. It depicts

the Nativity, Crucifixion and Resurrection as well as various saints. But the date was 1588, the year of the Spanish Armada, a time in our history when to produce such a strongly Roman Catholic style of picture for your local church could have been to risk your life. When you look more closely, however, you realise that the hinges of the doors look wrong; the doors have been turned inside out. This means that when the triptych was first hung in the church the more religious pictures of the saints and the rest would have been hidden and only revealed when it was safe to do so, while on the original outside cover there were simply portraits of members of the local Cornewall family.

While on the subject of decoration within churches there are also some fine examples of carved decorations to be found. I have already mentioned the carvings depicting the legend of Mitchell's Fold to be found within Middleton -in-Chirbury Church. The vicar, Waldegrave Brewster, was good with his hands and had time to spare. So he decided to carve the ends of the pews in his church. I hope his parishioners were happy – he used some of them as the models for his carvings. When he finished the pew ends he started on the rest of the church – scenes from the legend of Mitchell's Fold, zodiac signs – the whole church is covered with carvings.

Other interesting carvings can be found on St Swithin's Church at Cheswardine. They include a magnificent lion, a winged dragon, a Talbot and others and date from about 1470. The Talbot was a breed of hunting dog that has now died out but it was from them that present-day foxhounds were bred. It was also the badge of the Earls of Shrewsbury, and it's probably in this context that it appears here.

But a carving that particularly delights me is one on a pew done, presumably, by a bored child during a particularly long sermon. You'll find it in St Peter's Church in Melverley. It consists of a pattern of 33 holes just the right size for small marbles for playing games of solitaire.

Some unusual church furniture also survives: in Stokesay's church there is a reminder that the floors of country churches were seldom paved – if you look below some of the pews at the very back of the church you will see that they have little ledges so that people could rest their feet on these rather than directly on the damp soil.

When pews were first placed in churches, different families in the parish would often be assigned their own pews – in the church at Bettws-y-crwyn they even went to the length of putting the names of their farms on the ends of the pews.

Stokesay also has some fine Jacobean church furniture – box pews, an elaborate squire's pew and a double-decker pulpit. Another church with examples of these is St Mary's (left) at Longnor. The church in the village of St Martin's goes one better, however – it has a triple-decker pulpit although it has now been relegated to the back of the church.

Some odd items, other than furniture, can occasionally be found within churches. Maiden's garlands are a fine example. These are crowns that were used to adorn coffins at funerals, and were usually made of a linen-covered wooden frame which was decorated with coloured paper and ribbon, (and sometimes a paper pair of gloves was placed within the garland too). They would be made for a girl who was betrothed but never married because either she or her fiancé died before the wedding, and they were used to adorn the maiden's coffin at her funeral. After the funeral the wreath would be placed on her seat in the church. A maiden at such a funeral could be any age – a young girl who had died before her wedding or even an elderly spinster whose fiancé had died and to whom she then stayed true.

One maiden's garland (left) can be found in St Calixtus's Church at Astley Abbots – it was dedicated to Hannah Phillips who drowned in 1707 while crossing the River Severn on the eve of her wedding day.

But the best collection is to be found in Holy Trinity Church in Minsterley where there are seven garlands. When you first see them they are undoubtedly a disappointment – after 200 years of daylight and dust they've become faded and soiled and, to make matters worse, many have now been covered in polythene so that they're difficult to see – in fact, a modern one has recently been placed within the church to give visitors an idea of just what these garlands probably looked like when they were new. But the most amazing thing about these garlands is that such flimsy items have survived at all.

You can find strange things in churches sometimes – for example there's a ducking stool hanging on the wall near the entrance in St Peter's Church in Myddle. A ducking stool was really a chair attached to a pivoted post that would be held over a pond or river so that the victim could be dunked in the water. The poles that would once have been attached to it have gone, and actually it looks more the size of a child's high chair. Perhaps it was just used for naughty children – now, there's an idea!

PUBLIC BUILDINGS 6

Whitchurch
Prees
Oswestry
Weston-under-Redcastle
Wem
Shrewsbury
Telford
Horsehay
Boscobel
Ironbridge
Norton
Much Wenlock
Bridgnorth
Bishop's Castle
Morville
Alveley
Ludlow

Visitors who come to Shropshire for the first time are always delighted by the wealth of timber-framed, black and white buildings to be found all around the county. Living in the county, we soon become used to them, but there are many curiosities to be found in these buildings.

One thing that few people realise is that when people talked of moving house in the past they often meant it literally. As they were built of wooden frames with wooden pegs, it was a relatively simple task to dismantle these buildings and move them. Legend has it that the Town Hall in Bridgnorth is just such a building – the wooden structure sitting on the top is said to have once been a barn. Since the building was erected soon after a terrible fire that devastated the town during the Civil War in 1646, it's quite feasible that timber from other buildings around the region was used in order to speed up the rebuilding process.

Perhaps the best-known example of a building in Shropshire that has been moved to a new site is a private house, the Castle Gates House (above), that now sits beside the entrance to Shrewsbury's castle – it once sat in Dogpole.

In fact timber-framed buildings can be erected extremely fast. We're told, for example, that the Guildhall in Much Wenlock (opposite page, below) was built in two days – this seems incredible until you consider that the frame could well have been erected within two days – completion, however, would have taken rather longer. The speed with which such buildings were raised was due to the fact that the timber frames were always pre-fabricated in a carpenter's yard somewhere and not brought on to the site until everything was ready.

To make things even easier, the timbers were also numbered with Roman numerals when they were laid out in the carpenter's yards and it's still often possible to see these carpenter's marks. One of the best examples of a series of carpenter's marks can be found in Grope Lane in Shrewsbury, and the Liberal Club at the top of Belmont has another fine collection.

In the south of the county there are some clear carpenter's marks on the side of the House on Crutches in Bishop's Castle, which is a curious little building in itself. A common feature of timber-framed buildings is that the upper floors were often built to overhang those below – it was a way, after all, of obtaining additional floor space upstairs, and it is known as jettying. With this building this has been taken to such extremes that the upper floor is no longer capable of supporting itself on the floor below and so the *crutches* have had to be erected.

It's the detailing on these timber buildings that is often such fun. For example, when you have two sides of a jettied building meeting at a corner the technical term for the timber that links them is a *dragon beam* – thus in Mardol in Shrewsbury one delightful building actually has a carving of a dragon disguising the dragon beam.

Timber buildings of course are just perfect for displaying superb carving details, and in Shropshire these abound. Llwyd Mansion in Cross Street in Oswestry has a particularly fine double-headed carved eagle on the side. Apparently an early owner of the house was granted permission to use this symbol of the Holy Roman Emperor in return for services he rendered during the Crusades.

The Gate House to the former Council House in Castle Street, Shrewsbury is covered with delightful carvings including some mermaids, which always strike me as rather odd in this land-locked county. On the top of the gables there are two carvings, one of a man and the other of an old-fashioned form of key – said to be a reference to the fact that accused people coming to attend court here would have been imprisoned in the building while waiting for their cases to be heard.

Another favourite of mine is the carving that depicts Margaret Thatcher and Michael Heseltine on the building in the High Street in Shrewsbury at the bottom of Grope Lane. This is obviously a restored building with modern carvings on it but it shows that these old traditions continue right up to the present time. Incidentally, the date was that of Margaret Thatcher's resignation as Prime Minister.

Occasionally you'll find an odd piece of carved timber where you least expect it – next time you walk through Coffee House Passage near the Music Hall in Shrewsbury, look up – there's a beautifully carved beam there with the initials GP and the date 1577. It originally came from a house in Milk Street and was placed here when the other house was being renovated many years ago.

Another carving worth looking out for, although this time it's carved in stone, is the beehive above the entrance to Lloyds TSB Bank in Broad Street, Ludlow. Forget the black horse as the logo for this bank – the original Lloyds logo was the beehive, a symbol of making money through your own industry, and you can sometimes find these on older branches of the bank.

Nor is it only carvings that catch your eye – have you noticed the row of old meat-hooks above the ground-floor windows on the Abbot's House in Butcher Row, also in Shrewsbury? And, if you are in Ludlow look out also for the row of hooks on the ironmongers, Rickards & Sons, near the Bull Ring. Actually, the whole shop here is a wonderful reminder of what all our shops

were like only fifty or so years ago; it's a perfect time-capsule in itself.

There are dozens of curious little features adorning public buildings all around Shropshire. The old Market Hall in the Square in Shrewsbury, for example, has an old counting frame cut into the wall (left). No one knows for sure just how it was used but obviously the little holes would have had wooden pegs inserted in them for counting ... what? Wagon-loads of corn coming into and out of the market? Fleeces of wool or bundles of woollen cloth? We don't really know for sure.

Everyone trading in the markets would have had to pay a toll of some sort, and in Ludlow there is a reminder of this in a building that is still known as the Tolsey. It sits at the junction of Corve Street and Old Street, at just that point where people would have entered the market area between it

and the town's castle. It's a curious little building for another reason – it was once a court of *pied poudre*, a court of dusty feet. In other words it also served as a courthouse where people coming to market could air their grievances and get justice even before they had had a chance to get the dust off their feet. The types of cases heard in such courts were often those that could be dealt with quickly by local magistrates, such as boundary disputes between neighbours.

Of course where lots of people are trading there will often be disputes – traders accused of cheating or young boys attempting to steal the occasional loaf of bread. Such people would have quickly received justice, usually in the stocks where they would be pelted with rotten vegetables and goodness knows what else. Stocks, the word comes from *tree stumps*, were boards that clamped an offender's arms and legs and were a common form of punishment. At one time every parish in the country was supposed to erect a pair of stocks at its own expense.

One set of stocks can still be seen beside the church in Weston-under-Redcastle (above) and there's another in the village of Norton (below).

A particularly curious example of a place where such punishments were carried out is to be found on the Guildhall in the centre of Much Wenlock. Here there are two pairs of handcuffs (left) still attached to one of the posts on the front of the building.

Saddest of all though are the whipping posts because they were often used not solely for the deserving felon but also for those who had committed no crime other than to be destitute and in need of succour. When Henry VIII dissolved the monasteries he didn't just obliterate a few old churches; he also did away with an essential service that had been carried out by the church – the care and protection of the needy, the elderly, the infirm and the orphaned. Such people now became the responsibility of their local parishes where they were an unwanted expense, and the easiest way the parishes could avoid the expense would be to persuade such people to move elsewhere. And so, to encourage them to move on, they would be strapped to a whipping post, given a good beating and told to go. There's a whipping post in Norton, next to the stocks, and another in the village of Morville (left) beside the road junction.

Of course persistent criminals might require locking up, and for this purpose lock-ups were built. One still survives in the village of Prees – built in the 18th century it is thought to be one of only five lockups like it surviving in the whole country. Sitting just behind the buildings that front the street it is a cube of a building, made of sandstone with cornicing of a quality that you would expect on far grander buildings, the whole thing topped with an enormous stone ball. Today its appearance is totally ruined by a pair of corrugated iron gates that were attached to it sometime in the 20th century.

Many people who spent a night in the lock-up almost certainly arrived as a result of overindulgence in the local public house.

The oldest pub in the county is probably the Three Horseshoes in Alveley dating from the early 1400s. Not that it looks old. Like so many early timber-framed buildings, it has been covered with a later skin of brickwork. But it's another pub in Alveley (now a private house) that is particularly interesting – the former Bell Inn has, on its walls, some 20 carved stones which (so some say) may have been carved by our Anglo-Saxon or Viking ancestors.

You can find another example of ancient artwork inside the King's Head in Mardol, Shrewsbury. The medieval painting of the *Last Supper* on the old chimney breast within this pub dates from the 15th century and was later hidden under plaster. It was discovered when workmen started to renovate the building. Subsequently restored, it is a real treasure and leaves me wondering just how many other such treasures there are all around the country, hidden by subsequent alterations within the buildings or covered by Puritan zealots.

It wasn't just works of art that the Puritans wanted to destroy. They also sought out all Roman Catholics, and the priests who served them were particularly at risk. Priest holes were hiding places usually built within the walls of old buildings, and in the Bull Inn in Corve Street in Ludlow a priest hole has recently been discovered hidden within the ingle of the fireplace. Others can be found at Boscobel and these were probably used by Charles II, when he was on the run after the Battle of Worcester in 1651, as well as the more famous oak tree that I have already mentioned.

The Puritans also wanted to close down entirely those pubs that were used as brothels. There are one or two pubs along the Severn Gorge that claim to have been former brothels serving the men who worked the boats along the river – don't be misled, however, they probably all served this purpose!

There is though in Ironbridge one pub that was unlikely to have served as a brothel – it was built to attract a far higher class of clientele. The pub in question is the Tontine Hotel just next to the Iron Bridge itself and it was opened in 1783, having been built especially to accommodate the many

visitors coming to the area to see the Bridge. Its name is particularly interesting – a *tontine* is a special kind of investment whereby as individual investors in the business die their share doesn't go to their heirs but, rather, is returned to the business and the surviving investors. This arrangement is agreed beforehand in order to ensure that the business itself, after all but one of the original investors have died, remains in the hands of a sole proprietor rather than having to be broken up between any number of heirs.

Incidentally, if you stand at the southern side of the Iron Bridge and look across at the front door of the Tontine Hotel, you will only just see the lintel of the door. It's an indication of the stresses that the bridge itself has undergone since it was built when you realise that originally you would have been able, from the same spot, to have seen the whole door!

There are several curious names for pubs around the county one of which, in particular, is now considered to be politically incorrect – the Labour in Vain in Horsehay. An explanation of the name can be found when you look at the picture on the sign – a young black boy is sitting in the water of a village pump while the local people are labouring in vain to wash him white. Considered by many these days to be a slur on coloured people I see it only as a reminder of just how stupid some white people can be.

And while on the subject of pub signs – the White Horse pub in Oswestry may have closed long ago but its sign can still be seen in Church Street. It's a lovely sculpture of a white horse – but it only has three legs. The story is that, following a local election in 1832, a riot took place when an unpopular candidate was elected. One of the rioters climbed up to the horse, pulled its leg off and subsequently threw it through the window of the party offices of the successful candidate!

There are many old carved pub signs that survive long after the pubs themselves have disappeared. One particularly ornate sign is that for the old Buck's Head which still adorns a building in Mill Street in Wem (above).

Occasionally you will find buildings that seem to lean rather more than at first appears quite safe. One example is the old Tower on Shrewsbury's Town Walls (above right). It is the only one of several that once graced the medieval walls of the town. Today it sits just beside a busy road where the constant traffic has compacted the land on one side of the building to such a degree that the tower now leans slightly towards it.

But for a building that really leans quite alarmingly, go for a walk one day underneath Bridgnorth Castle – if you dare. The castle, or at least what remains of it, leans over at an angle of 17 degrees – that's considerably more than the Leaning Tower of Pisa! It has been like that since 1646 so you should be quite safe, but it's a strange feeling to walk under it.

The story is that the castle was held by Royalists during the Civil War, but was besieged by Parliamentarian soldiers who had taken control of the town of Bridgnorth. The Parliamentarians wanted to force the castle to surrender, but it was well stocked and the people within it were determined not to give in. Then the attackers came up with a brilliant idea – the castle sits on a very soft sandstone, and so they decided to tunnel underneath the castle, excavate as large a hole as they possibly could, fill that hole with explosives and blow the entire hillside (and the castle with it) to smithereens.

Fortunately for the men in the castle, they were warned of what was being planned and so they wisely surrendered. Consequently, only the castle was blown up and not the hill as well. The tunnel is known as Lavington's Hole after the man in charge of the digging. It's 70 feet (21m) long and the entrance, which is now blocked up, can be seen from Underhill Street.

CLOCKS 7

Since his early history, Man has wanted to measure time. Ancient astronomers measured the time between seasons, they knew when to be ready to plant their seeds and so developed zodiacal calendars.

With the advent of Christianity the measurement of time became even more important. People needed to know when particular days fell in order to worship correctly. And not just the days either – in the monasteries monks had to pray at set times each day and so it became important to measure the hours within each day as well.

An early form of clock was the sundial and there's possibly a very early one carved onto the side of St Mary's Church at Alveley (below left). A particularly beautiful sundial is to be found on the south-facing wall of St Bartholomew's Church at Benthall (below right).

Others were placed where the public could see them easily – there are fine examples in Shrewsbury on both the Library (above left) and the old Market Hall (above right).

For centuries the accuracy provided by sundials was as much as anyone needed. Not only that, but it didn't then matter that noon in London was several minutes earlier than noon in Bristol or Liverpool. Then, in the 19th century, the steam train was invented and before long there were railways criss-crossing the country. The efficient organisation of railway timetables required a system of telling the time and so Greenwich Mean Time became the basis for time throughout the country and clocks everywhere took their time from it – it even came to be known as "Railway Time". But of course this meant that all those sundials up and down the country were now incorrect. However, if you visit the church in Lilleshall you will see, just below the sundial, a bronze plate with lists of tables etched into it. These gave the number of minutes you needed to add to the time on the sundial at various times of the year in order to calculate Railway Time.

But the strangest sundial of them all must be the one in the car park area of the Madeley Court Hotel in Telford. It consists of an enormous cube of rock (about six feet high) with its sides facing north, south, east and west, each side being about four feet (1.2m) square. The north facing side is plain but on each of the other three sides there is a central basin-like indentation, surrounded by smaller, similar shapes so that there are 56 separate basins or dials altogether, some of which might have been purely decorative. In the middle of some of the basins there is a small hole which must be where the gnomon was originally attached.

It was probably painted in bright colours and it wouldn't just have told you the time either – apparently times of sunrise and sunset could have been worked out from this instrument, as well as signs of the zodiac and so on. It's thought to date from the late 16th or early 17th centuries and may have been installed here by Robert Brooke. Brooke was a lawyer and Speaker in the House of Commons who had bought the estate from Henry VIII in 1544 for the sum of £946. The sundial is, without doubt, a remarkable survival.

Reading such an astronomical toy would have been beyond the capabilities of most of us so that it's just as well that clocks with two hands began to appear on public buildings. Not that every clock in the county has two hands – the one on St Michael's Church in Lydbury North only has one. One-handed clocks date back to the time of Elizabeth I but this one was installed in 1728.

Most clocks are things that we take for granted, but there are one or two in Shropshire that are worth a second glance. Mind you, you would hardly need to look twice at the clock on St Agatha's Church in Llanymynech (right) – it's enormous and was deliberately made on such a large scale so that it could be seen by men working in the nearby quarry. Another clock that was positioned so that as many people as possible could see it was the one in the village of Knockin (below right) – it was placed over the entrance to the pub rather than on the church, as would be more usual, because the church is at the edge of the village where fewer people would have been able to see it.

A favourite clock of many people in the county is the one within the shopping centre in the middle of Telford (above) – children often gather just before the hour strikes in order to watch as the great frog blows his bubbles. At 17½ yards (16m) long, the clock is thought to be the largest indoor animated clock in Britain.

ANIMALS 8

In medieval times entertainment was often derived from cock-fighting, bear-baiting and bull-baiting and evidence of all these so-called amusements can still be found around the county.

Betting on the outcome of cock-fights was once a very popular pastime. The birds were especially bred for fighting and some even had sharp blades attached to their feet to help them when they attacked other birds. The fights were held in enclosed areas known as cockpits from which the birds couldn't escape (hence our modern term for a cockpit in an aeroplane). A couple of buildings that once housed cockpits still survive in Shropshire: there is one on a farm just outside Lydbury North. However another, more accessible, cockpit can be found on a hill behind the church at Beckbury. This one is thought to date from the 18th century and consists of a raised mound with a flat circular top some 7 feet (2m) across. It is said that this cockpit is one of only seven such examples in the entire country. Mind you, there is another explanation for this structure – some people think it is just a garden folly.

There's an old bear pit within the aptly named Bear Hotel in Hodnet where the poor animal would have been kept prior to being baited. Then in the village of Loppington there is actually a bull-ring in the middle of a road junction in the village. It consists of a simple iron ring stuck into the ground to which the animal would have been tethered and it's interesting to note that every time the road here is resurfaced the ring is removed prior to the work and then reinstalled. Local tradition

has it that the last time this bull-ring was used was in 1835 when a bear was brought along from Hanmer to be baited here as part, would you believe, of a wedding celebration. The vicar was appalled and put a stop to it. A more recent tradition is that if a man goes and turns over the ring he is throwing out a challenge to all-comers that he is the best man in Loppington.

But not every animal curiosity within the county has a cruel association. Next time you walk across a cattle grid stop and look to see if there is a small ramp within it – a special hedgehog escape ramp. These were the brainchild of Major Adrian Coles who, in 1982, founded the Hedgehog Preservation Society here in Shropshire. One thing the society tries to do is to encourage landowners to install these escape ramps into the pits so that those small animals, not just hedgehogs, that fall into them have a means of escape and won't starve to death.

Most curiosities associated with animals date back to times when farming and the rearing of livestock played a much more important part in our daily lives. Every town or village would have had its animal pound. Woe betide you if you let your animals stray, because they would then be caught and impounded (it's where the word comes from, after all) until you paid a fine to get them back. One or two of these old pounds survive. There's one in Much Wenlock right beside the road that leads from the town towards Shrewsbury. Others survive in Rudge and Wollerton, and in Caynham there is a plaque that recalls the old pound; another can be found near the church in St Martin's – this one is known locally as a "pinfold" rather than a pound.

Much Wenlock
Pound (above)

Rudge Pound
(right)

Wollerton Pound
(right)

Sometimes animals needed special accommodation – especially those that were introduced from warmer parts of the world to the cold British climate. Rabbits, for example, were introduced by the Normans soon after 1066 and were then considered an important part of the diet. Artificial burrows or warrens were dug for them and one such warren was so extensive that it's even marked on an Ordnance Survey map – although it is wrongly described on the map as "pillow mounds" (137 303988). This warren is to be found in the hills just to the east of the hamlet of Middleton-in-Chirbury.

A different form of accommodation, this time above the ground, was provided for doves and pigeons, again an important part of the medieval diet. At one time every lord of the manor kept his own doves or pigeons – not only were the birds' eggs a useful food source but also the birds themselves provided fresh meat during the winter. But it was only the lord of the manor who could keep these birds; this meant an additional hardship for the lord's tenants, as his birds ate their seeds and fresh shoots in the fields while they were not allowed to kill or even scare them away. It was only in 1761 that a law was passed enabling anyone to keep a dovecote.

Many dovecotes were built into the sides of barns and their distinctive pattern of holes in the brickwork can often be seen. Monasteries all used to have their dovecotes, too, and it's thought that the Elizabethan dovecote at Whitehall in Shrewsbury probably once stood on the site of an older one that would originally have belonged to Shrewsbury Abbey. Others survive in the grounds of a number of houses around the county. One of the finest, and certainly the most easily accessible for visitors, is the one at Shipton Hall with nestholes for 400 birds.

Perhaps the quirkiest of them all is the pyramid-shaped dovecote (right) near Tong (127 783076). It was built by the famous landscape gardener, Capability Brown, as one of several follies when he was landscaping the grounds of the now demolished Tong Castle. Not just a dovecote, the lower part of the structure also served as a henhouse, and the building still retains its old roosts and ladders.

Rabbits, doves and pigeons are still with us – mammoths are not. The skeletons of a group of these animals were discovered in the gravel pits just outside the village of Condover and, since their discovery in 1986, these animals have been displayed in many parts of Britain before finally finding a permanent home at the Discovery Centre in Craven Arms. One of the mammoths looks extremely realistic but its fur is fake. If, on the other hand, you want to see genuine old animals visit Hodnet Hall where there is a magnificent display – a fine example of the taxidermist's art. There are animals from all around the world adorning the walls and display-cabinets of the tea room. Perhaps not everyone's choice as décor, but I find them quite fascinating.

Finally, there is even a curiosity associated with bees at St Bartholomew's Church at Benthall. Look closely at the lion's head just below the sundial on the church. At one time bees used to enter a hive kept within the church through a hole in the lion's mouth. The honey they produced was then given to the local poor. Incidentally, St Bartholomew was the patron saint of bees, which makes me wonder which came first – the bees or the dedication of the church.

9 BORDERS & BOUNDARIES

Knowing the boundaries of your own territory and protecting it from incursions has always been important since man first laid claim to his own patch of forest for hunting or his own stretch of river for fishing. Consequently there are many curious features around the country that are associated with the marking of borders and many of them date back to very early times.

One of the best known in this area is, of course, Offa's Dyke. Offa's Dyke was dug to indicate the position of the border along the western side of the kingdom of Mercia.

King Offa, who gave his name to the dyke, lived at the end of the 8th century. He was an extremely powerful king and a contemporary and rival to Charlemagne. Under him the little kingdom of Mercia grew from being only one of several kingdoms to become the most important in all of Anglo-Saxon England.

The dyke consists of a ditch and earth bank, the earth dug from the ditch forming a rampart along one side, so that the whole structure from the top of the rampart to the bottom of the ditch was originally over 25 feet (7.6m) high. Furthermore, the dyke snakes over the border hills and valleys for a distance of around 77 miles (124km). It's the magnitude of the entire system that astounds me. It was built within only a few years by men working with picks and shovels in what we still insist on calling the Dark Ages. In the centuries since it was built, the border has been shifted many times so that the dyke no longer defines the line between England and Wales. One place, however, where it still forms the English-Welsh border is between Chirbury and Montgomery and this is also a particularly fine section to study as well as being easily accessible.

But Offa's Dyke isn't the only boundary or boundary marker of interest in Shropshire. Mind you, the others are all rather smaller – generally parish boundaries. Stone boundary markers for various parishes can be found all over the place and as such should never be moved. One that *has* been moved is the one the defines the boundary between the parishes of St Julian's and Abbey Foregate in Shrewsbury – this large stone used to sit on one of the mud banks in the middle of the river but can now be seen on the town side of the English Bridge.

Another parish boundary stone can be found in Mill Street in Whitchurch. It has been built into a house sitting beside the road, and the letters "W" and "D" indicate the parishes of Whitchurch and Dodington with a line showing the exact position where the two parishes meet.

Back in Shrewsbury, another boundary stone sits in the middle of the grass area in the Quarry Gardens. It's known as the Harley Stone because it was used as a boundary marker by a family of that name. They owned some of the land here and refused to sell it in the 18th century to the town's Corporation when the rest of the Quarry was being acquired to develop pleasure gardens, and so the stone marked the boundary of their land. Incidentally, the Council paid the Harley family 4 shillings and sixpence a year as rental and this continued until at least 1875.

Most boundary markers were large stones, their very weight making it difficult for them to be moved. Occasionally trees would also serve this purpose but this could cause problems when the trees reached the end of their natural life span. Presumably it was one such tree that led to a forked pole being used as a boundary marker on Titterstone Clee. Known locally as the "Three-Forked Pole," it marked the meeting point of three parishes on the top of the hill. Every 30 years or so when the pole decayed a new one would be put in its place. No one knows when the first pole was erected although photographs record one early replacement ceremony in the 1920s.

Some boundary stones marked the limits of towns. In medieval times it was often the custom, when celebrating the saint's day of a local church, for parishioners to walk to the edge of the town and gather before parading back into the town. One such marker stone could be the Croeswylan stone in Oswestry (also known as the "Cross of Wailing") that sits beside the road to Morda. As they processed into the town some in the crowd would flagellate themselves and weep and wail as they went, so that a number of these meeting places are commemorated in the name Weeping Cross. There's one such place-name to the south of Shrewsbury and another on the eastern side of Ludlow.

One or two boys would have wept and wailed on occasion in the village of Norton in Hales. For here there is another stone, in this case sitting on the village green. It's known as the Bradling Stone and is another glacial erratic, like the Belstone mentioned earlier.

Traditionally, on a set date each year, the children of the parish would "Beat the Bounds" walking to each of a number of such stones around their parish, banging their heads against the stones as they went. This was to teach them to know their own territory – perhaps a rather brutal method but surely effective!

Over time this tradition changed, and eventually it became the rule that any man or boy in the village who was found working after noon on Shrove Tuesday would be "bradled" – in other words have his head banged against the stone on the green.

There are also a number of boundary stones around Shropshire that are linked to large estates. One that is relatively easy to find is near to Thresholds (137 413996) on Long Mynd (right).

Borders have a tendency to be arbitrarily defined lines linking places, and they often totally ignore what is happening on the ground. Sometimes borders cut right through properties, even through houses. One interesting example of this was in the former Lion Hotel beside the A483 in Llanymynech. The true position of the English/Welsh border used to be marked on the wall in the bar. This proved to be extremely useful in the days when drinking hours in Wales were much more restricted than those in England. On Sundays, when all the pubs in Wales were closed, the drinkers here only had to make sure they were on the English side of the room in order to be able to continue buying their drinks!

Another building which had a border going right through it had a great financial advantage for the local girls. It was a cottage on the parish border between Cold Weston and Stoke St Milborough, and it's said that it was used as a retreat for unmarried mothers in the 19th century. When the house was visited by the local overseer coming to offer financial assistance to the girls, the girls would move to the side of the room that was in whichever parish the overseer represented in order to claim whatever money they could from him. Benefit cheating isn't new!

Finally, if you enjoy a game of golf, perhaps you should go to the Llanymynech Golf Course – there you can stand with one foot in England and the other in Wales as you strike your ball on the fourth tee.

ALONG THE ROADSIDE 10

As we drive around the countryside we often pass curious little relics from bygone times. Sometimes it is obvious what we are looking at but some relics are a bit more unusual.

Milestones used to be exactly that, stones erected every mile along a toll road so that travellers could tell exactly where they were. Shropshire is rich in both the number of milestones that survive and in the variety of their styles. The simplest ones, perhaps, are to be found in the area around Bishop's Castle. These are, as their name suggests, made of stone. Others are made from iron – some of Shropshire's finest iron milestones are situated along the route of Thomas Telford's Holyhead Road, much of which today overlaps with our modern A5.

Incidentally, it's interesting to note that on many of these milestones Shrewsbury is referred to as *Salop*. Many people today assume that the word Salop is simply an abbreviated form of Shropshire, but, until relatively recently, it also served as a shortened form for Shrewsbury as well.

A standard milestone will just tell you the distance between two towns linked by the road you are travelling. But some milestones give you far more information than you could possibly want on a single journey. There's just such a milestone in Shrewsbury sitting beside the roundabout at the top of Abbey Foregate next to Lord Hill's Column. But the finest milestone in Shropshire has to be the one by the road junction in Craven Arms where the A49 and the B4368 meet (left): this one gives you mileages to towns and cities all over the country – 295 miles to Edinburgh, 136 miles to Holyhead and 7½ miles to Ludlow, for example. However, for sheer accuracy, the milestone in Abbey Foregate, Shrewsbury, would take some beating: "County Hall: 6 furlongs 174 yards".

Milestones shouldn't be confused with signposts; the first tell you the distance to a place, the second point out the direction in which you should travel to go there.

One particularly delightful little signpost stands by the road junction in Little Brampton on the B4368. The post is made of stone but the individual arms are made of iron with, in each case, the name of the town cut out of the iron. The towns on the sign are Ludlow, Bishop's Castle and Clunn (no, that is not my spelling mistake, that's how it is spelt on the sign).

All these milestones and signposts date from the great age of road building in the 18th and early 19th centuries when stagecoach travel was at its height. Some of the roads from that period were particularly well-made and you had to pay for the privilege of using them; you did this by stopping and paying at tollhouses along the way and a number of these survive, especially along the Holyhead Road. There's one fine example beside the bridge in Montford (right).

Another tollhouse from the Holyhead Road is one that people can now visit. It used to sit in Shelton on the outskirts of Shrewsbury but has been moved and refurbished and can now be found in the Blists Hill Victorian Town near Ironbridge. Even the short stretch of road just beside this restored tollhouse has been built in just the same way as Telford would have built his original road in the early 1800s.

While on the subject of Thomas Telford, a modern curiosity is the artwork that dominates the roundabout at the point at which the old A5 road from London enters the modern town of Telford in Priorslee. I include this as one of my curiosities because most people either just ignore it or dismiss it as a weird example of modern art without ever questioning what it portrays. The sculpture depicts Thomas Telford's mason's mark. As a young boy learning his trade in Dumfriesshire in the mid 1700s, Thomas would have signed his work with a chiselled mark and would then have been paid according to the quantity of work he'd proved he had done. So this is not just another example of weird modern art – it does have a story to tell.

Thomas Telford has become very much an adopted son of Shropshire. But a genuine son of the county has a most unusual roadside monument: I'm talking of Admiral John Benbow. Benbow was born in Shrewsbury in 1651 and joined the Navy. Tradition has it that when he left his home he attached his door key by a nail to a tree but he was away from the town for such a long time that by the time he returned the tree had partially grown over the old key. Benbow's key is now housed in a glass-fronted cabinet in front of the apartments at Benbow's Quay (a pun that delights me), on Chester Street in Shrewsbury.

Many roadside curiosities are there because they were built to serve travellers using the roads. For example, the many drinking troughs for cattle were there for animals that would have been herded along these roads while on their way to market. One such drinking trough that I particularly like is the one on the A49 in Craven Arms – on it are written the words "Be kind and merciful to all animals".

It's not just animals that need a drink. Sometimes humans want one too, and to serve this need drinking fountains were erected. One or two survive, although these days the water source has invariably been turned off. One example is the old drinking fountain on the side of the Town Hall in Bridgnorth. There are also a number of village pumps that survive although many have been moved in recent years to become mere garden ornaments. One in its original position survives beside the medieval tower on Town Walls in Shrewsbury.

However there is one place where the passing traveller can still stop to get a drink – All Stretton on the B4370. Stretton Hills mineral water is well-known, and at the entrance to the bottling plant there is a tap above an enamel sink from which passers-by can fill up their water bottles. The incongruity of this enamel sink in the middle of the stone wall beside the pavement and next to a busy road, always strikes me as most amusing.

Have too much to drink as you are travelling and you might need to relieve yourself. In the village of Minsterley you didn't need to go behind a hedge, or at least the gentlemen didn't – there's a wonderful old Victorian pissoir, as they were called, right beside the roundabout in the centre of the village. This one was made by a company of ironmasters in Glasgow, McFarlane's. They had a catalogue of iron products that ran to 4,000 items and the pissoir would have been delivered in its separate iron components to be erected on site. Look, too, for the little sign inside the pissoir reminding gentlemen to "adjust your dress before leaving".

Just as today, people used the roads to travel to and from markets and many indications of these markets still survive. The most obvious such survivals are the old market crosses. Far from being purely decorative, market crosses had a serious function. The earliest markets would usually have been held in churchyards – people coming to attend a church service would, while they were in the town or village, also attend the market. Yes, even on Sundays. In fact many people don't realise, when they argue about Sunday trading these days that we have come full-circle – many markets were originally held on Sundays until a pope around the 12th century banned such Sunday trading.

Whether on Mondays or Tuesdays or Saturdays or Sundays, the earliest markets were held in churchyards – a convenient place where people congregated in the centre of the community. Within these small markets people would trade and make verbal agreements – "If you bring along a pig like that next week I promise I'll pay you a penny," or whatever the going rate was. In a society where most people were illiterate, such agreements were never written down, but as they were made in the churchyard, in God's acre so to speak, He was there to ensure that both parties kept their word.

As time went by and markets grew both in size and in the variety of products sold, new markets were established in areas away from the church. But what was to happen in such places when traders now made agreements? Crosses, as symbols of the church, were then set up in these new markets to ensure that all agreements there still had a definite legal validity. Which is why there are so many medieval market crosses to be found all over England.

Not all market crosses are in the centre of communities – one such relic with a particularly sad association is the Buttercross to the north of the village of Alveley (right). This cross stands about six feet (2m) high next to what is now a very minor country lane, and the possibility that this was once a market place at first seems quite absurd. It dates back, however, to a time when plagues were a constant threat – at such times people were far too scared of infection to meet in large groups in their usual markets, but they still needed to buy and sell their produce. Thus markets were established in areas away from the community where people could leave their goods so that others could come along at another time and purchase, leaving their few coins, often in a bowl of water or vinegar to avoid infection.

The Croeswylan stone in Oswestry (pictured on page 65) is also said to have served this purpose, and some people have suggested that the hollow within the stone was not the base for a standing cross at all but was merely a receptacle for holding coins in liquid of some sort.

Other associations with early markets are tollhouses such as the Tolsey in Ludlow, which I mentioned earlier. Tolls were usually payable at certain points of entry into the town, and a rather beautiful tollgate sign, known as "The Newgate Pillar", survives in Oswestry on Church Street (left).

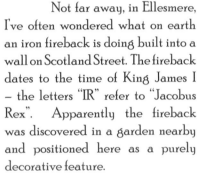

Not far away, in Ellesmere, I've often wondered what on earth an iron fireback is doing built into a wall on Scotland Street. The fireback dates to the time of King James I – the letters "IR" refer to "Jacobus Rex". Apparently the fireback was discovered in a garden nearby and positioned here as a purely decorative feature.

As you walk along streets in Shropshire's towns, you will often come across what I call "pavement oddities" – the street furniture of former times. These include the old boot-scrapers just beside doorways, or sometimes they are even cut into the wall of the building. Beside them you will occasionally find the entrances to old coal cellars. When, in the 18th and 19th centuries, coal was delivered to households it was tipped down a chute directly into the cellar below. In Ludlow there are some particularly pretty coal cellar covers decorated with what appear to be daisies.

In Shrewsbury, if you look at the pavements as you walk along, you may notice here and there a little silver footprint. These are Brother Cadfael's footprints. They were inserted into the pavements as markers of trails for the many tourists who come to the town having read the *Brother Cadfael* detective novels written by the Shropshire author, Ellis Peters.

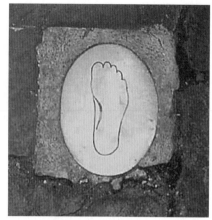

ODD SIGNS 11

Never automatically believe what you read, even when the plaque or sign appears to be official and knowledgeable. There's a plaque, for example, on the English Bridge in Shrewsbury that tells us that Queen Mary opened the newly restored bridge in 1927. But she didn't do anything of the sort.

It so happened that the Prince of Wales (the future Duke of Windsor) was due to come to the town to open the bridge but, following the death of a minor member of the royal family, all the family went into mourning and their public engagements for a short time were cancelled. Who could be asked to open the bridge at such short notice? Then people remembered that not long before, Queen Mary had been visiting the town privately and, although the bridge was still being repaired at the time and was closed to traffic, special arrangements had been made so that she could cross the bridge in her car. It was therefore decided that, by crossing the bridge, Queen Mary had thereby reopened it.

And so we read on the sign that Queen Mary opened the bridge but, in fact, she was totally unaware of the fact at the time and so were all the other people who were present at the "opening".

Speaking of bridges, at the other side of Shrewsbury on the Welsh Bridge, there's a sign that always amuses me. It simply reads "Commit no nuisance".

Shropshire has some delightful placenames guaranteed to make you smile. How would you like to live in The Bog? Homer sounds very classy, but I'm not too sure the same can be said for nearby Wigwig. And what does one buy in The Knockin Shop?

Street names, too – I particularly like the sound of the Ding Dong Steps in Broseley. Possibly the name derives from the sound made by all the people wearing wooden clogs with studs in the soles as they walked up and down. As for the meaning of Grope Lane in Shrewsbury – well, just don't ask!

Then there's New Invention – what was the invention that gave that little hamlet its name? Stories vary. Some say it concerns King Charles I, but, so far as I'm aware, he was never in the area. Others say it's about Charles II when he was on the run following the Battle of Worcester. He was making his way from Worcester to France, but he wasn't exactly using the shortest route since he certainly travelled through Shropshire. But this does seem a little out of his way, even so. Yet others say the story concerns the highwayman, Dick Turpin, but since he terrorised travellers along the London to York road this, once again, seems a little bit unlikely.

Whoever it was, the man was being pursued on horseback when he reached the little hamlet in the valley and discovered the blacksmith working there. He went and asked him to remove all the shoes from his horse and then replace them back to front. Job completed, the man remounted and rode away. His pursuers, following his trail, reached the hamlet and tried to work out which way he had gone but now all the fresh trails led into the valley and none of them led out. And so, whoever it was, he got away. And if you believe that, you'll believe anything!

Another sign that delights me is the little plaque on the gate leading into the churchyard at Melverley, which tells us that the village was "Britain's most motivated village" in the year 1991. It's a fascinating story. The little timber church was originally built in 1406, an earlier church having been burnt down by Owain Glyndwr. On visiting this church you will see that it sits on a little hillock just beside the River Vyrnwy. However, any time it and the nearby River Severn flood, the whole landscape here changes as the water invades. Constant flooding over the centuries had affected the solidity of the ground here to such an extent that the little church was in danger of being washed away. In order to save their church the parishioners needed to raise £250,000. The restoration was a major project in itself as the entire church had to be raised aloft, like a car on jacks, while a solid concrete foundation was inserted below. Once this was completed the church was replaced on its new secure, rock-like base. Safe, we hope, for the next 600 years. Motivation indeed.

And lastly, does the "Last Day" in Oswestry indicate the end of the world? Not at all. Apparently, it was first painted, many years ago, by a schoolboy at Oswestry College to celebrate his last day at school. Since then it has been repainted each year by whichever departing schoolboy has been at the college for the longest time. It may say "Last Day" but I think for the schoolboys who paint it each year, it is much more likely to celebrate the beginning of a new life.

12 EARLIEST HOUSES

People have always needed shelter from the elements and protection from wild beasts and, perhaps, their fellow men. In the earliest days such shelters were frequently to be found within caves and, here in Shropshire, cave dwellings were used until well into the 20th century. Some of the finest examples are still to be found in the hillsides around Bridgnorth. One cave, known as the Hermitage (138 728935), gets its name because, so legend has it, a grandson of King Alfred, Aethelward, lived here as a hermit in the early 10th century. This cave was occupied until 1928 and is a great one to explore because, although not deep, it's still easy to see it as a house with its doorways, stairs and shelves.

The soft sandstone has led, over the years, to the creation of numerous large, manmade caves all around Bridgnorth. There are even a number in the heart of the town along the Cartway. These old homes have been blocked up, but other former dwellings survive, usually as stores, workshops and even garages. With their constant temperature at all times of the year, these were such excellent places for storage that at one time Bridgnorth was renowned for its "cave ales."

Another cave with an interesting story is the one at Nesscliffe (126 384193). This cave was once the hideout of Shropshire's own Robin Hood – Humphrey Kynaston. Kynaston was a local nobleman from Myddle Castle who murdered a man in Church Stretton in 1491. He went on the run, hiding with his horse, Beelzebub, in this cave and became an outlaw preying on rich travellers as they passed along the nearby roads. But, since he shared some at least of his takings with local poor people, he soon became something of a hero in the region. Eventually, in 1518, Henry VIII gave Kynaston a free pardon, and he spent the rest of his life in peace on a small estate near Welshpool. He died in 1534.

Other early houses include squatters' cottages and there are a number of examples of these within Shropshire. The tradition was that people could lay claim to a property provided they had, in the space of one night, erected a house with a hearth and had a fire burning in it by dawn the following morning. Consequently, what happened was that a number of people would get together and prepare everything they would need; as dusk fell they would set to work erecting a house of sorts. Provided there was a roof over the structure by morning and a fire burning in the hearth the family could lay claim to the site and, having claimed the site, they would then slowly complete their house.

Being built by only the poorest members of society many of these would have been very flimsy shanty-like structures, built using whatever materials were freely available. Some were eventually completed in stone, and it is these houses that survive, if they survive at all. One such squatters' cottage has now been moved to the Blists Hill Victorian Town in Telford, and it is hard to imagine how a family of probably three generations with numerous children could have managed in this two-room hovel.

Another similar cottage can be found on Smithfield Road in Much Wenlock – this one was reputedly occupied by a witch in the 1800s. She was named Nanny Morgan and was famous for the love potions she supplied. This little cottage is still occupied.

Of course none of these houses would originally have had modern plumbing or bathroom facilities. Instead you would have had to use the privy at the bottom of the garden, and many of these survive. There are several examples at Blists Hill.

Using the toilet is an essential part of everyday life, and one or two interesting examples of toilets survive. Perhaps one that will always amuse children is the old toilet or *garderobe* in the Shrewsbury branch of McDonald's on Pride Hill. This was built into the old town walls and now serves as a small eating area, though few of the people who use it are aware of its original purpose. Incidentally the old name *garderobe* simply means wardrobe in French – in other words a garderobe was where you kept your clothes. Why keep your clothes in such a place where they would be bound to get smelly? The point was that it was the very smell of the ammonia from the urine that kept the moths away. What people smelt like as they dressed in their best clothes on a Sunday morning to attend church, one can only imagine!

If you go for a walk around the outside of Ludlow Castle and look up as it towers above you, you will see the sluices for a number of garderobes easily visible (left). At Boscobel there are three old privies, two of which have been restored. You could sit and have a friendly chat in these – they are two-seaters. But for real communal toilet facilities the ones at Haughmond Abbey would have been best – there, there is an 18-seater, although it's difficult today to really picture it as only the drain survives to show where it once was. This one is said to be haunted by the monk who used to clean it out – he can still be seen endlessly pushing his wheelbarrow of muck.

LATER 13
DOMESTIC
BUILDINGS

Of course the glory of Shropshire's domestic buildings is to be found in the many timber-framed houses around the county. These come in all shapes and sizes, some were very large and grand, others tiny. The oldest such house in the county, perhaps one of the oldest in the country, is Cruck Cottage in the little village of Upton Magna. It was recently restored and, while this was being done, the timbers were dated and it was discovered that the house was erected around 1260.

Cruck houses are amongst the earliest type of timber houses to survive anywhere in the country, and we have a number of them here. Another example overlooks the large roundabout in Frankwell in Shrewsbury. Cruck houses have a distinctive frame, and the way in which they were constructed can best be understood when you look at the gable ends of these buildings.

When these houses were being built, people would first go into the forest to select suitable trees – trees with a straight trunk and one branch going off at an angle of about 45 degrees. This angled branch would then be sliced down the middle and the two matching pieces would form the outer frame of the building. Similar timbers would then be used at intervals along the building with the crucks (the word is perhaps derived from *crooked*) held steady by horizontal timbers along the length of the building. Such a building could be as long as you liked – there's even a terraced cruck house in Barrow Street in Much Wenlock but, unfortunately, it has long since been covered with a stone frontage so that the cruck timbers can only be seen from within the houses.

Although a cruck house could be any length its width and height were obviously limited by the size of the timbers used. Eventually the technology of building timber houses changed to box-frames, and, with this system, a house could be built to any size, so that cruck houses soon came to be associated with housing for the poorer people in society. By the late 1500s we see the glorious timber buildings that are the reason why so many people, when they see any timber buildings, look knowledgeably at them and describe them as Tudor buildings. But in fact, many so-called "Tudor" buildings that survive around the county are much earlier.

Timber buildings were replaced by the brick buildings with which we are so familiar – the style of building that we now describe as "Georgian" that is typified by the elegant styles which prevailed in England in the late 18th and early 19th centuries.

To tell the truth many Georgian buildings are no more Georgian than the earlier Tudor buildings were Tudor. With the introduction of brick, many people, who already had perfectly good timber houses felt they were somewhat old-fashioned. How could they keep up with those of their neighbours who were building fine new, modern, elegant, brick houses? Easy! They could build a brick façade over the front of their old house to disguise it and so keep up with the neighbours without all the expense of a total rebuild.

Houses disguised in this way can be found in almost any town in the country, and we have some fine examples in Shropshire. One of the best has to be the Liberal Club in Belmont in Shrewsbury (opposite page). If you stand directly in front of this building it looks a perfect example of a three-storey 18th century brick mansion. Move slightly to the side of it, however, and all is revealed – it is actually a large timber house with a brick façade.

Occasionally, when fake facades were erected to cover old walls, they didn't even bother to use proper bricks. There was no need, after all, since the building already had a perfectly solid wall. Instead tiles, made to look just

like bricks, would be used. It was a cost-cutting exercise since producing and transporting such tiles was far cheaper than the heavier bricks. These fakes are known as *mathematical tiles* and finding examples of them is an almost impossible task since they were produced deliberately to look like bricks, and no-one would want to be seen as a cheapskate by giving the game away.

However, there is one house where the plaster used to disguise some mathematical tiles has worn away so that the tiles can be seen – and this is Attingham Park in the village of Atcham. The front of this house is extremely grand with its Grinshill stone façade, but money was saved on those walls facing the internal courtyard, which wouldn't have been seen by the ordinary visitor to the house. Nowadays visitors to the house, which is a National Trust property, are allowed upstairs and it is from one of the upstairs windows that you can see the mathematical tiles.

Another curiosity to be found in the same house is its picture gallery or, at least, its skylight. This is a wonderful reminder of the way that technology was changing at the time. It was just after he had returned from a Grand Tour in Europe that the second Lord Berwick, owner of Attingham Park, decided that he needed a large gallery in which to display all the treasures he had acquired. So in 1805 he asked the architect, John Nash, to design one for him, and Nash chose to construct it in the heart of the building. This, however, presented the problem of how he was to bring light into a room that had no exterior walls and his solution was to build a skylight.

The skylight was made of a grid of curved iron braces running along all four sides of the roof, into which were fitted the panes of glass. But, as with so many innovatory ideas, it didn't quite work – apparently the skylight leaked almost from the day it was made – but the idea caught the imagination, so that within a short time it was being copied by people like Joseph Paxton, who was to build the conservatories at Chatsworth House in the 1830s and, of course, later designed the Crystal Palace. Incidentally, it wasn't until the National Trust built a completely separate skylight over the original one at Attingham that the weather was finally kept out. Meantime, there are many positions within the present picture gallery where, when you look up at the skylight, you can easily see the gaps in the roof.

Another feature of Attingham Park, one that can be found in many houses around the county, is that not all of its windows are genuine – some are blocked up sections of wall made to look from a distance like normal windows. An important aspect of buildings from this period is that their design was symmetrical, so that there was always an equal number of windows balancing each other on either side of the front door, and it's easy to find examples where one of these is a blocked-up or fake window.

Many people take one look and announce knowledgeably, "Ah, window tax windows!" but that's not necessarily the case. The window tax was introduced in the 1690s, whereas most of these houses were built in the 1700s. Why deliberately construct a building knowing that you are immediately going to want to block the window to avoid paying the tax? You will often find that these fake windows have been painted, complete with fake white glazing bars between the supposed panes of glass, so that it's only when you look at them carefully that you realise they are fake. What was happening was that these windows were there simply to retain the building's overall symmetry. One of the best examples of a house with windows blocked up merely to retain the symmetry is the Old Vicarage on Church Street in Madeley (top, opposite page). This house has twelve windows on its front elevation, yet only two of them are genuine.

Of course many older buildings do have windows that were blocked to avoid paying window tax. Insofar as any tax can be considered fair, I suppose the window tax was fair – those people who had the largest houses with

therefore the most windows in their houses would invariably have been the people with the most money who would have been taxed accordingly. The interesting point is that the size of each window was irrelevant – it was the total number of windows in your house that you were taxed on.

Consequently, you then find houses where people have built large windows serving more than one floor in order to try and beat the taxman. One wonderful example of such a building is in Ludlow beside the market square. This building has just one window on its side wall, but that one window lights up the entire stairwell over several floors. This house was actually built in the 1830s and, since the window tax was abolished soon afterwards, there is now a dispute as to whether this could really be described as a window-tax window. Personally, I like to think that the man who had this house built was just being careful – he may well have known that the tax was about to be abolished but would he be prepared to trust the government, any government, not to reintroduce the tax later when it needed some extra cash? I'm sure he was playing safe!

Another way of playing safe and protecting your house was to buy insurance. In an age when most of the buildings in our towns were made of timber, the risk of fire was always present. There were no municipal fire services as we have today. Consequently, from the late 1600s people began to establish their own private fire services as a form of early house insurance. A modern analogy would be a small co-operative society with individual members paying subscriptions to run a private fire service and give cover for insurance payments in the event of a fire. To show that you were a fully paid up member of such a club, you had a badge to display on the wall of your house – a fire insurance plaque.

Then, in the event of a fire, you could send a servant racing to the fire office to summon help to put the fire out; the fire officers would arrive, look at the front of the building to check that you were indeed a paid up member and proceed, you hoped, to put the fire out before too much damage was done. In fact, because of the way in which fires can spread so rapidly, your insurance cover would also mean that the fire services would be prepared to help extinguish your neighbour's house should it be the one to catch fire rather than your own.

Once the idea had taken hold, these insurance companies began to be established all over the country so that the different badges of the different societies can be seen everywhere. Here in Shropshire the two main companies

were the Shropshire and North Wales and the Salop Fire Office.

Looking at these badges today and considering them as curious survivals of a bygone age, it's interesting to reflect that all these little companies still exist. Consider the possibility – a fire is blazing and you send your servant to the fire office but he runs to the wrong office and so the officers turn up at your door, look at your badge and say, "Oh, no, wrong company. Nothing to do with us, mate. Sorry." And your house subsequently burns to the ground.

It's not difficult to imagine that, following such a disaster, members of both companies would have met and come to an arrangement to put out each other's fires with the costs being assessed afterwards. That would be your first merger. Over the three hundred years that have passed since these companies were first formed many mergers have taken place so that, today, all our major insurance companies can trace their origins to these early companies and, in that sense, they do indeed still exist.

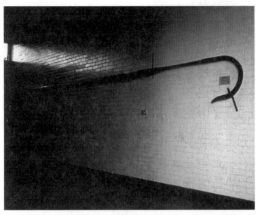

While on the subject of fires, there's an oddity to be found in Wem – an old fire hook. An important aspect of controlling the spread of a fire in the past used to be by the drastic method of using a long hook to pull down thatched roofs, and sometimes even houses in the path of a fire, in order to try and limit the fire's spread. The fire hook is displayed along the wall in the fire station in Wem – it's some 20 feet (6m) in length and is extremely heavy and unwieldy. It was used, unsuccessfully, to try and prevent the spread of the Great Fire of Wem in 1677.

Insurance plaques, fake windows, facades and quaint timber buildings are all relatively common throughout England. There are, however, some curious features of individual houses that are worth noticing. In Ludlow, for example, Broad Street epitomises everything that was elegant and smart about Georgian England – but here, too, there are some unfortunate details. Have a look at Number 18 on the eastern side of the street – those two doors spoil the entire line of the building. The man who once lived here ran his business (a private bank) from his home. Apparently his wife didn't like the prospect of all her husband's clients walking through her hall to see him in his office, and so she insisted on having that ugly secondary door inserted into the building and there it has remained to this day.

Further down the same street, but on the other side of the road, Number 7 at first appears to have elegant, if rather over-ornate windows. But look closely at the top of the windows and you'll see that the tops are all fake, because the ceilings of the rooms are all slightly lower than the height of the windows.

As one moves around the county there are many houses with unusual details to be seen. As I drive along the A49 through the village of Felhampton, for example, I always look out for the bell on the top of Felhampton Court. It was used to call workers in from the fields at the end of the day or for their meals.

Another house, this time with curious carvings, is Benthall Hall (opposite page). Now owned by the National Trust, it dates from the 1580s. This was a period of terrible religious persecution when it was dangerous to show your allegiances to the Roman Catholic faith.   As priests travelled the countryside, they needed to know which houses would offer them safe refuge. The Benthalls, owners of this house, were Roman Catholics and they used these secret symbols on the outside of Benthall Hall as an indication of their religious beliefs. They can be seen just above the main entrance and

are said to represent the stigmata or wounds that Jesus suffered at His crucifixion.

Finally, another unusual house is Bedstone Court in the village of Bedstone. It was what's known as a calendar house built towards the end of the 19th century. The building is now part of Bedstone College, and I doubt whether it still has its original 365 windows for the days of the year, 52 rooms to symbolise the weeks and 12 chimneys, one for each month.

14 GARDENS & GAZEBOS

Today everyone with pretensions to grandeur wants a house with a fine garden and, hopefully, a gazebo or summer house. This is nothing new. The word gazebo comes from the Latin meaning *I will gaze* and this was their original purpose – somewhere pleasant to sit, away from the hurly-burly of a busy household where you could admire the garden and perhaps a fine view.

One particularly pretty little gazebo is Laura's Tower in the grounds of Shrewsbury Castle. It was built by Thomas Telford in 1790 and was a coming-of-age gift to the daughter of William Pulteney (Shrewsbury's MP at the time),

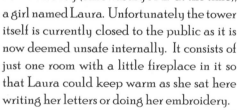

a girl named Laura. Unfortunately the tower itself is currently closed to the public as it is now deemed unsafe internally. It consists of just one room with a little fireplace in it so that Laura could keep warm as she sat here writing her letters or doing her embroidery.

Another, much larger, and also older, gazebo is the Banqueting Hall near Eyton-upon-Severn (126 573061). Despite its grand name this is more like a gazebo since, as a true banqueting hall, it would have been difficult for many people to partake of a large feast inside it.

In fact, such places were often just used only for the dessert course of a grand feast. This one dates from the late 16th century: it's a two storey structure and has recently been restored by the Vivat Trust, so that it is now used as the most delightful accommodation for holiday lets.

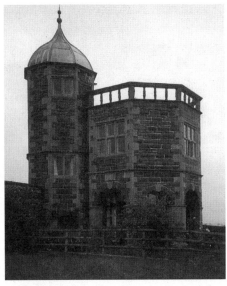

Not all gazebos are covered structures. At Boscobel House a special raised mound with a planted arbour was built, from which you could sit and admire the garden around you. Consequently, this was a garden designed to be seen from above with its rows of plantings specially designed to be admired also from the upper storeys of the house.

Another place in which to escape from the house and view a garden is in a tree house. The best known tree house in Shropshire is in the grounds of Pitchford Hall. It was built in the 1690s and must be one of the oldest tree houses in the world. Sitting in a large lime tree, it is a little black-and-white timber structure with a solid oak floor and pretty little gothic windows, which were probably inserted when it was altered at some time in the late 1700s. Its main claim to fame is that Queen Victoria, visiting Shropshire as a child in 1832, played in "the little house in the tree" and commented on it in her diary. Incidentally, she also described the main house in her diary as a large "cottage"! Unfortunately, the tree house is on private land and so is not accessible to the public.

Another structure, this time usually built into the ground rather than on or above it, was the icehouse. Icehouses, the first walk-in freezers, became popular in the 17th century and soon wealthy landowners were building them on their estates. These structures are really large underground holes, usually lined with brick. During the winter months ice would be cut when the local ponds froze over, and then packed into the icehouses from where, over the next few months, it would be delivered to the kitchen as it was needed. When you consider the state of the pond water, it was hardly a very hygienic source of ice. With the introduction of fast steam ships in the 19th century ice began to be imported from Norway and even from as far away as North America until, when ice producing machines were invented, this trade and the need for icehouses came to an end.

An interesting example of an icehouse in Shropshire can be seen in the grounds of Attingham Park in Atcham. There are, in fact, two icehouses here: the earlier is a simple brick-lined pit; the later (and more elaborately constructed) icehouse has been restored by the National Trust and is open to visitors. Unfortunately this icehouse was built rather close to the river and would have been liable to flooding, not exactly the best conditions for storing ice. Consequently, it was used for only a short time before being converted for use as a pump house supplying water to the main house nearby.

Whitchurch
Whixall
Oswestry
Newport
Longdon-on-Tern
Shrewsbury
Coalbrookdale
Telford
Madeley
Pitchford
Ironbridge
Coalport
Morville
Bridgnorth
Bishop's Castle
Ludlow

Perhaps the most interesting oddity in all of Shropshire is something that today we all take completely for granted and don't find in the least unusual. I'm speaking of the Iron Bridge at Ironbridge, even the town beside it is now known by its bridge. However, when it was first built the bridge was considered so strange that people travelled from far and wide, quite literally from around the world, to see it.

These people marvelled when they saw the bridge, for such a large structure in iron had never been seen anywhere before. No-one was terribly sure whether it was safe or whether it would survive the vagaries of the weather.

Then in 1795, less than twenty years after it was built, there was a terrible flood. Bridges all along the River Severn from Shrewsbury to Worcester were damaged, and many were washed away. The only bridge totally to withstand the flood was the new iron one, so that, overnight, people came to realise that such a bridge was sound. Within ten years the technology of building iron bridges was being copied everywhere.

In fact, this first bridge should more accurately be described as a wooden-iron bridge. Let me explain: it's understood that the bridge was designed by Thomas Farnolls Pritchard, a man whose trade had originally been carpentry. Consequently, when asked by Abraham Darby III to design this bridge, Pritchard's design followed the technology of carpentry – all the joints on the bridge are mortice-and-tenon or dovetail joints. Pritchard, however, died before the bridge was constructed, and it is likely that his design had been altered to some degree by Darby, who better understood the material with which he was working. Nevertheless, it's as though a wooden bridge was designed, wooden pieces were carved, moulds were made from these wooden pieces and iron then cast in these moulds –thus it is indeed a wooden bridge made of iron.

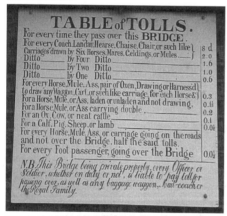

The bridge opened to the public on 1 January 1781. It was a toll bridge, and the little building on the south bank of the river is the old toll house on which are displayed all the rates to be paid. Note that, being a private bridge, even members of the Royal Family were expected to pay when they used it; this tradition was remembered when Queen Elizabeth paid a penny to cross the bridge when she visited Ironbridge during her Golden Jubilee tour in 2002.

Another particularly pretty iron bridge in the county is the Cantlop Bridge (126 517062) near Pitchford. This dates from the early 1800s and is the only one of Thomas Telford's iron bridges still *in situ* in Shropshire.

To us, the Iron Bridge symbolises the Industrial Revolution of the 18th century. It was here in Shropshire, in Coalbrookdale, where the whole world was changed by Abraham Darby III's grandfather, Abraham Darby I, when he discovered a technique for using coke to smelt iron-ore rather than wasteful charcoal. Today that part of Telford that includes Coalbrookdale and Ironbridge down to Jackfield and Coalport is a World Heritage Site and is full of reminders of all that happened here. Even the kerbstones in Ironbridge are made of iron.

But the effects of the Industrial Revolution were felt all over the county, and curious reminders of that period are to be found everywhere. As soon as it could be produced in large quantities, iron was used in all kinds of ways – before long it was replacing wood in buildings, and being used for window frames. There's a fine example of iron windows in the building that now houses the Museum of Iron (below) in Coalbrookdale itself. Another particularly beautiful set of iron windows can be found in St Alkmund's Church (right) in Shrewsbury – these have been recently re-cast and look quite stunning.

Iron was soon being used also for decoration on buildings. One lovely example, with marvellous decorative iron scrolls running across the façade, is on Shrewsbury's Pride Hill (right) and there's another pleasing use of iron for decorative windows in the High Street in Whitchurch (overleaf).

Wrought iron can be twisted into beautiful patterns and is often used for the production of decorative gates – one of my favourite examples in Shropshire is a gate at the entrance to Aldenham Hall (below left) just outside the village of Morville. Notice the leg in the centre of the gate – there is a delightful story associated with this. Apparently, so the story goes, many years ago the original owner of this estate was told that he could have as much land as he could walk around in one day. He set off walking as dawn broke and so acquired an enormous stretch of land.

The sun was beginning to sink and he was rather pleased with all his efforts. And then he noticed a large field just across the river. Oh, how he wanted that field too! He looked at the setting sun. There was no time to get across the river and claim it. What was he to do? So he chopped his leg off and threw it across the river. The leg landed neatly in that field, he could claim to have set foot in that field before the sun set, and so he acquired it as well. And indeed, if you look closely at the leg on the gate you will see that there are drops of blood falling from the thigh.

If you hadn't the room to build a grand gateway, another way in which to make an imposing entrance for your house was to have a colonnaded porch. Just such a porch with iron columns was added to Newport Place in Dogpole in Shrewsbury. There are quite a few private houses in Shropshire that have iron columns by their front doors. Of course, sometimes the iron columns are part of the structure of the building. I have already mentioned the iron columns used in the building of New St Chad's Church, also in Shrewsbury.

Sometimes a wander around a churchyard will lead to the discovery of iron tombstones or even entire box tombs. One of the best examples is the tomb of John Fletcher (left). A well loved preacher in 18th century Shropshire, John Fletcher was a close friend of both John and Charles Wesley. His tomb is to be found in the churchyard of St Michael's Church in Madeley and a wander around that churchyard will reveal other examples too.

Perhaps some of Shropshire's oldest iron tombstones are those in St Leonard's Church in Bridgnorth – these have now been brought within the church and date from the late 1600s. Incidentally, notice the date of Thomas Stedman's death on one of these tombstones – 29 February 1707.

The first iron railways, the first iron wheels, the first iron boat were all produced in Shropshire. These may not survive, but there are other firsts that do – the world's first multi-storey iron-framed building, for example, can be found in 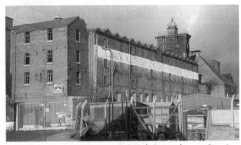 Shrewsbury overlooking Spring Gardens. Ditherington Mill (above) was built in 1796/97 as a flax mill, the idea being that (with no timber in the structure) it would be fireproof.

The Industrial Revolution would never have been successful had it not been for a revolution in methods of transportation that took place throughout Britain at the same time. I have already mentioned the 18th century toll roads because of the numerous signposts and milestones associated with them. Another revolutionary change was the introduction of canals. Canals had been around for some time, but the earliest ones were really ordinary river routes that were widened or deepened to allow for regular river traffic.

The first proper purpose-built canal was the Bridgewater Canal opened in 1761 to serve Manchester. Before long others were built all over the country. It was here in Shropshire, however, that the world's first iron aqueduct for a canal was built. Today it looks  totally incongruous – what appears to be an iron bridge sitting in the middle of nowhere straddling the River Tern just beside Longdon-on-Tern (above) (127 617156). It was built in 1796 by Thomas Telford, and although one assumes he had the backing of local ironmasters when he made it, most people took one look and said, "It'll never work – as soon as there's a heavy frost, the water will turn to ice and the stress will cause the whole thing to crack."

But "most people" were wrong. It was a success and it is quite likely that when this was built Telford was proving a theory because, within the next ten years, he was to build the two aqueducts for which he has always been famous – the one crossing the border near Chirk and his masterpiece in Wales, the Pontcysyllte Aqueduct.

Another feature of the canals, unique to Shropshire, is the design of the lift bridges to be found along the Ellesmere Canal, now part of the Shropshire Union Canal system. A fine example can be seen near Whixall (126 492346).

The route of a canal is of course dictated by the topography of the land through which it travels. Occasionally canals have to go up and down hills and so locks were built to control the levels of water along the route. Moving the narrowboats up and down flights of locks was and is an extremely time-consuming business, and many methods, including aqueducts, were used to overcome this problem. One place where this puzzle was solved in a most unusual way was at Coalport. Here the problem was how to link the Shropshire Canal (not to be confused with the much later Shropshire Union Canal) with the River Severn, some 120 feet (36.5m) below – a height that would normally require the building of 27 locks.

The problem was solved by building the Hay Incline (127 695027). It consists of two parallel sets of railway tracks which, despite their appearance, did not carry trains but, rather, two tub-like boats sitting on wheeled cradles. They always worked in tandem so that, as one boat was carried down to the bottom of the hill another boat would be lifted as a counterbalance up to the top. It was built in 1793 and worked admirably for around 100 years. There were about 20 such inclined planes built around the country, six of them in Shropshire. The last one in use was finally closed in 1921.

Locks however were easier to use for large numbers of laden boats. An unusual form of lock was the guillotine lock which had gates that rose vertically and this style of lock was designed by Telford for use on the Shrewsbury Canal in order to save water when small numbers of boats were using it.

The remnants of one such guillotine lock can still be seen in Hadley Park (127 672133) in Telford. It underwent some restoration in the 1970s but, sadly, is in a state of disrepair once again.

One final curious feature of the canals is the roving bridge. When building canals, the engineers tried where possible always to keep the towpath on one side of the canal so that the horses pulling the narrowboats could walk steadily without changing direction. When the towpath changed from one side to the other, the horse would have to be untied, walked across the bridge and then hitched up again in order to continue. A roving bridge seems a rather odd shape until you realise that it was designed so that the horse could cross the bridge without having to be untied or become entangled in any way. Walk across such a bridge, pulling an imaginary boat on an imaginary rope, and you will see exactly what I mean. There's a fine example of such a bridge at Lower Bar (below) in Newport.

16 OTHER INDUSTRIAL SURVIVALS

Not all our industrial oddities are associated with the changes brought about by the Industrial Revolution in the 18th century. We have many reminders that industrial activity in Shropshire has been ongoing since prehistoric times, such as the lead ingot in Linley Hall, near Bishop's Castle. The Hall is privately owned, but if you ever get the chance to visit, look out for the ingot – it dates from Roman times when lead was being mined in the Stiperstones hills, and it requires at least six people just to lift it.

The whole area around the Stiperstones was mined for lead for centuries, the industry only dying out in the early years of the 20th century. No-one in those early days thought of green issues, and so the spoil from the mines was just dumped anywhere. This has since led to problems of regeneration in the area because of the high arsenic content of the spoil. Another reminder of this old industry is the presence of two engine-house towers (137 319980 and 137 327992) either side of the A488 between Minsterley and Bishop's Castle.

At nearby Snailbeach there is another curious building associated with the old mines – a dynamite store (126 378023). Breaking up the rock for the mines required large quantities of dynamite, and this needed to be stored somewhere safely. It's a little cube of a building with thick, dense walls. The doorways don't face each other either, so that to enter the building you need to walk along a small maze, and then there seems to be little evidence that there was any roof on it. Actually, there would have been a roof but it was deliberately built to be flimsy. The idea was that, in the event of an explosion, the roof would be blown off and the strong walls of the structure would force any explosion upwards rather than outwards. Snailbeach is well worth a

visit for anyone interested in our industrial heritage; remains of the old lead workings are all around the village.

Further evidence of early industry can be found for example in the lime kilns (138 586977) set back from the road along Wenlock Edge – these can easily be viewed from the National Trust walk that has been laid out here.

Another industrial curiosity can be seen inside a pub – the Kynnersley Arms in Leighton. The pub sits astride an old waterwheel that was built to power an early corn mill and, later, an iron forge – apparently cannon balls were amongst the things made here during the time of the English Civil War. The pub achieved national fame recently when the landlord invited Tony Robinson and his Channel Four *Time Team* along to investigate the history of the building.

Shropshire is, however, predominantly a rural county and many of the old industries reflect this. There's a water powered mill at Daniel's Mill, Eardington which is still used to mill grain. Said to be the largest water-wheel in Britain, it has a diameter of 31 feet (9.4m) and weighs some 31 tons (28,000kg).

Another important local industry was tanning. Hides had first to be soaked for long periods, and many a village pond would have been used for this purpose. The hides were then hung up to dry, and it was important at this

stage that the air moving around them should as constant and as even as possible. Sheds built for the purpose, therefore, often had slats built into their sides in order to control the movement of air, and one building where these slats still survive (although they have long since been nailed solid) is in Noble Street in Wem.

Wem has another odd claim to fame, with its treacle mines – not something that we can see today, although there is a sweet shop in the town that uses the name. Presumably this tradition for treacle mines came about because of the combination of two industries in the town, tanning and brewing, both of which would have produced a thick, gooey, syrupy waste. Perhaps someone once tasted the mixture and liked it and so the legend started. Of course, a similar product came from the brewing industry in Burton with the production of Marmite!

Some curiosities associated with travel in the past include the many ferries that used to operate all along the River Severn. Indeed, it is said that the ferryman who was put out of business by the building of the Iron Bridge was the only person who was subsequently given permission to cross the bridge free of charge whenever he wished. Of all the old ferries, only one service survives – at Hampton Loade. There has been a ferry crossing here since possibly the

16th century when it served local farm and forge-workers. Today it is mostly used by ramblers and cyclists exploring the Severn Valley. It's a chain ferry – operated using a wire rope stretched from one bank to the other with a pulley attached. The ferry is tethered to the pulley; when the rudder is placed in position a sideways force is created due to the current of the river and the boat then drifts across the river.

Reminders of the presence of many more of these ferries can be found at points all along the river in the form of the old posts to which the ferry ropes were tied – an example can be seen in the Quarry Gardens in Shrewsbury.

Finally, with the introduction in the 1800s of the railways, Shropshire became important as a junction for lines from north and south linking with lines between England and Wales. As a result Shrewsbury became a major railway junction with up to 180 or

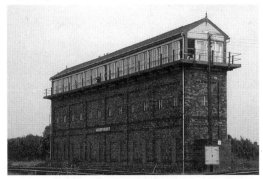

200 passenger trains stopping here each day. Organising these, and all the freight trains that travelled through the station as well, required an efficient system of signals, and today the signal box controlling the lines through Shrewsbury station is the largest manned signal box anywhere in Europe, all others having since been computerised.

It's not just the signal box that's interesting. Shropshire also has another curious type of railway surviving – the cliff railway at Bridgnorth. Opened in 1892 to link High and Low Town, this is now the only surviving inland cliff railway in Britain. Not only that but it also has the steepest and shortest incline of any cliff railway in the country. When it was opened a single ticket cost just one penny.

17 THE TWENTIETH CENTURY

20th century oddities, being recent, and therefore better understood by us, are much harder to find, if only because we don't see them as odd. But there are one or two and, as memories of the Second World War rapidly recede, most of the 20th century oddities in this collection are associated with that period in our history.

Shropshire was hardly on the front line, yet the presence of numerous old pill boxes dotted around the county reminds us that fears of an invasion in which enemy soldiers could be air-lifted into any part of England were very real at the time. Today, when one comes across these relics, it is difficult to imagine them as continuous lines of defence protecting the country, but one or two seem to have a more obvious purpose. There is one in Stafford Street in Market Drayton (below left), for example, which is obviously guarding the canal there. Another, near the village of Cressage (below right) (126 594044), however, seems to sit in the middle of a field with little purpose, although one can only assume it was there to control the nearby bridge crossing the River Severn.

The purpose of the pill boxes seems evident, but building a tank trap in Ellesmere strikes me as over-cautious. The evidence of it is still there, in St John's Hill. Notice what look like squares of concrete on the road. These are the filled in remains of holes cut into the surface of the road where once, in an emergency, metal barriers could have been hastily erected.

It is when you visit the area between the villages of Kinnerley and Nesscliffe that you begin to understand the military role of the county of Shropshire during the Second World War. The county served as one enormous storehouse. Everything was held ready here – tanks, food, planes, ammunition, even people... One important ammunition store was in the old quarry workings on the top of Brown Clee Hill near Ditton Priors, but the largest ammunition dump in the whole country was the one near Nesscliffe where numerous purpose-built ammunition stores (such as the one pictured below) were built.

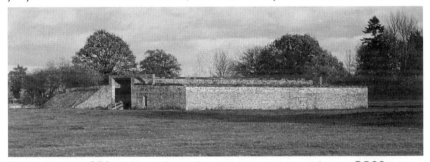

There are over 200 of them altogether covering an area of some 2,500 acres. They are all huge hangar-like sheds built of concrete and brick, sometimes with earth embankments around the sides. Like the ammunition store at Snailbeach, the roof of each structure was relatively flimsy so that, in the event of an accident, any blast would be forced upwards.

Another Second World War site, associated in this case with D-Day preparations, is the old testing site at Ebury Hill (126 545165) (which, incidentally, has another military connection since it is also an ancient Iron Age hill fort). Now a peaceful camp site, in the months leading up to D-Day this was a military testing site for armoured personnel vehicles known as Universal or Bren Carriers. These tracked vehicles were manufactured at the Sentinel Wagon Works in Shrewsbury, and their design needed to be modified so that they could be driven through the water on the Normandy beaches. The quarry at Ebury Hill, along with its concrete ramp into the lake, was used for testing them. This is a rare example of a specialised military establishment, much of which survives virtually intact within the present caravan park.

Coming right up to date, we have the golf ball (138 598779) that sits on top of Titterstone Clee Hill. At least, from a distance it looks just like a golf ball sitting on its tee waiting to be struck. In reality, however, it houses an air-traffic surveillance radar centre, not only controlling the movement of planes around the globe but also used for meteorological research.

FOLLIES 18

When we consider oddities of any period in history, we tend to find ourselves looking at things that were of use, or at least had some meaning, to people at the time they were built. Follies, however, don't come into this category at all. They are, as their name suggests, merely the foolish whims of the people who built them. It was in the 18th century, when the owners of large mansions began to landscape their parklands, that it became fashionable to build within those parks structures whose sole purpose was to adorn and catch the eye as part of the picturesque landscape.

One such area of parkland in Shropshire has since become particularly famous for its collection of follies – Hawkstone Park at Weston-under-Redcastle. The follies here all date from the 18th century and by the Victorian era Hawkstone had become a popular tourist resort. Apparently it was particularly popular with honeymooners – it must have been romantic wandering along the footpaths through the open woodland and every now and again coming across a picturesque little folly.

Sadly, most of these follies subsequently became extremely dilapidated and then, when the park was used to house a Prisoner of War camp during World War II, many were further destroyed. In the 1990s the park and follies were largely restored, and today the site is, once again, a tourist attraction. There are many types of follies here, including a narrow cleft through rocks that leads to a grotto which was once completely covered with sea shells (unfortunately it would have been too expensive to restore this).

Like Hawkstone, another folly recently restored is Flounders Folly (overleaf) (137 460850). This is a tall, 80 feet (23m) high tower that sits on

the highest point of Wenlock Edge overlooking Craven Arms. It was built in 1838 by Benjamin Flounders, probably as a boundary marker, certainly as a viewing tower. A legend grew up, however, that Flounders, a wealthy shipping magnate, built the folly in order to see his ships coming into port. Whether the port in question was Liverpool or Bristol, either way Flounders would have had to have had remarkable eyesight not only to see the port but also to see through the hills that block the view in both directions! Like those at Hawkstone, this folly also became extremely dilapidated and dangerous. The central stairwell was damaged, and the entire shell was on the point of total collapse when it was restored at a cost of over £300,000. It was reopened in 2005 by the Princess Royal, and visitors can now climb it and admire the views once again.

The people who did most to make follies fashionable in the 18th century were members of the nobility and gentry who had been on The Grand Tour. On their travels they had seen wonderful ruins of Roman and Greek architecture, and this influence is often found in the follies they then built on their estates once they returned to England.

Follies with a distinct *Greco-Roman-ruin* look about them, can certainly be found in Shropshire. One such example is the set of columns beside the A442 at Hodnet (below left) – this folly was positioned so that it was on the skyline when you looked away from the front entrance to Hodnet Hall, as though to give the impression that there had once been a Grecian temple nearby. Another Grecian temple was built in Badger Dingle (138 772994) near Beckbury (below right) – this one was a complete building, designed by James Wyatt, and has since been restored and renovated by the Vivat Trust.

Going even further back in imagined time, we have a prehistoric Stonehenge folly at Weston Rhyn (126 280364). Not as large as the genuine article in Wiltshire, this is obviously modelled on the real Stonehenge with

stones placed horizontally across uprights. Unfortunately, some stones have fallen, revealing that, instead of the carved stone mortice and tenon joints used at Stonehenge, here they were originally attached to each other with large metal pins which rather spoils the exotic look of the stone circle.

Not all follies are totally without purpose. One in the village of Hadnall is big enough to be used as a private house. It's a fake windmill (126 523210) and was erected by Lord Rowland Hill. Lord Hill fought at the Battle of Waterloo alongside the Duke of Wellington and later decided to commemorate the battle by building this replica of a windmill that stood on the battlefield site. How accurate a representation it is, I do not know, but it certainly serves today as a delightful little cottage.

Another folly which had a secondary purpose was Haughmond Castle (126 536138). Built in the late 18th century, this was originally used as a signal tower to alert huntsmen of forthcoming foxhunts in the area. Much of it collapsed in 1931 so that today only part of its base survives, comprising a rubble-built wall the stones of which are held in place by iron bands.

19 AND FINALLY SOME UNUSUAL GRAVES & MEMORIALS

Whitchurch •
Welshampton •
Moreton Say •
Stoke-upon-Tern •
Cockshutt •
Oswestry •
Clive •
Haughmond •
Shrewsbury •
Telford •
Coalbrookdale •
Tong •
Church Stretton •
Shirlett •
Bridgnorth
Bishop's Castle •
Bettws-y-crwyn •
Ludlow •

Churchyards can be treasure trove sites for those of us who collect oddities, whether it be the tombs themselves or, quite often, the memorials on those tombs. One or two memorials can be quite funny, I assume unintentionally. There's one, for example, at Church Stretton dedicated to Ann Cook who died in 1814. The inscription reads:

> *On a Thursday was born*
> *On a Thursday made a bride*
> *On a Thursday broke her leg*
> *And on a Thursday died.*

Those who study family history are soon taught that they should never automatically believe everything they read on a tombstone. Sometimes errors creep in, and this, surely, is the case with a tombstone on what I call the Leap Year grave in the churchyard of All Saints Church in Clive. It's the date that must be wrong because the inscription tells us that Thomas Green died on 29 February 1835!

Another memorial that always makes me smile is to be seen inside St Leonard's Church (left) in Bridgnorth. It's on the north wall of the chancel and is dedicated to the memory of a lady called

Dorothy Shepperd, who died in 1706 and is described as "a discreet woman". It always leaves me wondering what it was that she was so discreet about – was she good at keeping her friends' secrets? Or was it perhaps the infidelities of her husband (or even herself) that made her discretion so important?

In the churchyard outside St Leonard's there's another unusual tomb – it's a stone coffin with the inside of it hollowed out to make space for the body. These were a common feature for the well-to-do in medieval times – another example can be found in the churchyard of St Julian's Church in Shrewsbury, and there's another in the Chapter House at Haughmond Abbey.

Tradition has it that William the Conqueror's body was placed in just such a tomb when he died in 1087. Apparently, the tomb was put in position in the cathedral in Caen, William's body was brought in reverent procession and placed inside the coffin, and it was only at this point that it was realised he was too big for the cavity. So there and then, in full view of the congregation, some of the monks climbed on top of him and tried to squash William's body into the tomb by stamping on it. In doing so they broke his ribs, one of which then punctured his stomach. The resulting stench caused the entire congregation rapidly to vacate the church.

Such tombs, of course, required lids and some stone coffin lids, dating from much the same time, lie on the ground in the churchyard against the north wall of at St Peter's Church in Stoke upon Tern.

In one special case it is the cemetery itself that is unusual – I'm referring here to the Quaker burial ground in Coalbrookdale (below). Quakers regarded all humans as equal in God's eyes and refused to refer to people according to their rank or title. This extended to their treatment of the dead so that many Quaker cemeteries didn't allow tombstones and, where they did, they were always made in an identical style and bore only the name of the deceased and the date of death. The stones that line the walls either side of the cemetery record several generations of, for example, the Darby family.

Not all graves are in cemeteries. In one example in Shropshire there's an old tombstone miles from any church – it's the Cantlin Stone (137 202869) near Bettws-y-crwyn in the hills in the far south west of the county. On the stone are written the words "WC died here 1691. Buried at Bettws". The "WC" stands for William Cantlin. William was a tramp whose body was found at this spot which is where two parishes meet. The people from the two parishes then argued as to which parish should have the expense of burying the poor man. Bettws-y-crwyn lost the argument and paid up for his burial but, in the meantime, also had enough spare cash to place this stone on the spot. Nearly 200 years later, during the reign of Queen Victoria, forestry workers came to the area to plant out trees and wanted first to map out exactly which bits of ground belonged to which parish. Since William had died at this place and was buried in Bettws this area of land therefore obviously belonged to the parish. So you could say that two centuries after their good deed the people of Bettws eventually got their reward. William Cantlin: there is a local tradition that no-one ever knew William's surname and that the word *Cantlin* is actually derived from Can't tell. Certainly the words sound very similar when spoken in the local dialect.

On the other hand, in St Michael's Church in Welshampton we do have a name, a most unusual name – Jeremiah Lebopena Moshueshue. He was an African prince from Basutoland (modern day Lesotho) visiting England to study theology and he died while he was staying here in 1863.

A much more famous person was Robert Clive. The victor of the Battle of Plassey in 1757, he was thereby the man who ensured that India became part of a British rather than a French empire. But Clive died in mysterious circumstances. In all probability he committed suicide, but the horror and shame of such an act ensured that everything was done that could be done to prevent the true facts from becoming known. It must be remembered that in those days people who committed suicide were still usually refused a religious funeral or even permission to be buried in a churchyard. It is a measure of the power (and wealth) of Clive's family that they managed to arrange to have a proper funeral, even though it was held at night with only the immediate family present. Consequently, no-one was ever told afterwards exactly where the grave was; nor was there a proper gravestone. Instead a small memorial was placed on the wall of St Margaret's Church in the village of Moreton Say to indicate that Clive lay nearby.

We all love our pets, and there must be many of us who have buried pets in our gardens; sometimes we may even erect small memorials to them. There's one memorial in a private garden near Cockshutt that recalls a very special dog indeed. His name was Rob and he was one of the first animals to be awarded the Dickin Medal, the animal Victoria Cross. Rob served with the SAS on campaign in North Africa and Italy during World War II. He made over 20 parachute jumps and worked behind enemy lines, sometimes for weeks at a time, and his ceaseless vigilance for his team of human soldiers undoubtedly saved many of them from discovery and subsequent capture or death.

On the other hand there's a very grand memorial to a dog in Shirlett Forest (right) (138 665977), although these days it's hidden away in the forest and you virtually need a machete to get through the undergrowth to find it. It's a tall obelisk built to commemorate a retriever that died as a result of falling down an old mine shaft in the area.

I would like to finish by mentioning two more graves – both of which recall people who never even existed. The first is in the churchyard of New St Chad's Church in Shrewsbury. Half way down the churchyard there is a tombstone with the name "Ebenezer Scrooge." Placed there in the 1980s, it was used for the scene where Scrooge is shown his own grave in the film version of Charles Dickens's *A Christmas Carol* starring George C Scott as Scrooge.

Charles Dickens travelled widely, giving readings from his books to the public and collecting, as he did so, plots and ideas for his books. In another of his books he set part of the story in Shropshire – in Tong to be precise. The book was *The Old Curiosity Shop* and it was in Tong that Little Nell finally died and was laid to rest.

Then, as now, people who read the story decided they would like to visit the places that the book described, and before long, people were flocking to see where Little Nell had been buried. The verger at St Mary and St Bartholomew's Church was no fool and realised that there was a nice little earner, as they say, to be made from these visitors. Consequently, he prepared in the far corner of the churchyard a grave and, when people arrived and asked to see Little Nell's grave, the verger would say, "Yes, come along. I'll show you where she lies." He would show his visitors the grave and meekly put out his hand for a reward, and he earned quite a few pennies in this way.

Then he began to get a bit old, his joints stiffened up and he didn't want the trouble of walking all the way to the bottom of the churchyard. And so he moved the grave. Afterwards, he would sit in the porch of the church and, when visitors came along looking for Little Nell, all he had to do was point to the grave and put out his hand and still receive a penny for his trouble.

To this day, when you visit Tong's churchyard, you will find Little Nell's grave just beside the path that leads to the church porch.

Why not go and have a look for yourself!

Dorothy Nicolle will tell you that she has the perfect job - she lives in Shropshire where she is a professional (Blue Badge) tourist guide for the Heart of England region. This means she can constantly share her love of exploring Britain and it's history with visitors and local people alike.

She also lectures on a variety of subjects and is particularly interested in the hidden history of subjects we otherwise take for granted - pub signs or nursery rhymes, the English language or even Christmas. This book has been written in response to many requests, following her talks, that she should write a book about the diverse collection of oddities scattered across the Shropshire landscape.

Amongst her hobbies and interests Dorothy enjoys walking and this has led to her writting a book on *Shropshire Walks with Ghosts and Legends* and she is currently walking the walks for another such book. She has also written over a dozen books for the Frith Book Company - these are photographic histories using pictures from an archive of photographs dating from the 1800s. Her most recent book, however, is a book on Christmas called *All About Christmas*. It explores why we celebrate Christmas in the way that we do and explains how many of the pagan traditions associated with Christmas came about.

To discover more about Dorothy's books, lectures and tours visit **www.nicolle.me.uk**